DON CARL[OS]

Opera in Four Acts

Music by

Giuseppe Verdi

Libretto by
JOSEPH MERY and CAMILLE DU LOCLE

English Version by
WALTER DUCLOUX

ED. 2712

G. SCHIRMER, Inc.

7777 W. BLUEMOUND RD. P.O. BOX 13819 MILWAUKEE, WI 53213

Copyright © 1958 by Walter Ducloux
Copyright assigned 1963 to G. Schirmer, Inc.
Printed in U.S.A.

46224cx

Note

All rights of any kind with respect to the English translation and any part thereof, including but not limited to stage, radio, television, performance, motion picture, mechanical, printing, and selling, are strictly reserved.

License to perform this work in this translation in whole or in part must be secured in writing from the Publishers. Terms will be quoted upon request.

G. SCHIRMER, INC.

DON CARLO

La grande boutique, the big shop, as Verdi called the Paris Opéra, played a significant role in the composer's life. He often criticized that institute, whose cumbersome administrative apparatus and archaic ways made a bona-fide dramatist like Verdi cringe in frustration. Yet it was the leading opera house of what was undeniably the cultural capital of the mid-nineteenth-century Western world, and no composer could afford to ignore the prestige of being performed there. In turn, the Opéra needed the genius of the man who, with Meyerbeer gone and Wagner not yet at the pinnacle of fame, was the most renowned opera composer of the day, Verdi.

Spending the winter of 1865-66 in Paris, Verdi agreed to writing a new work for the Opéra. Having previously used three plays by Schiller as a source for libretti, he again turned to the German playwright. This time, his choice was the idealistic and powerful *Don Carlos.* The French libretto was to be written by an experienced if not particularly distinguished author, Joseph Méry. When he died before finishing the task, the libretto was completed by Camille du Locle, whose qualifications included the fact that he was the son-in-law of M. Perrin, the general manager of the Opéra.

Work on the opera at first proceeded easily, until political events interfered. War broke out between Italy and Austria, and Verdi had to leave his beloved home and favorite place of work at Sant'Agata near Parma. Depressed and discouraged, he asked for a release from his contract. When Perrin refused, the composer finished the score while taking a cure in the Pyrenees. The premiere had been planned for the fall of 1866, with rehearsals starting in September. Verdi, as always, supervised the production himself. Soon enough, the usual tribulations began to appear: Illnesses, strikes, and a general lack of sympathy for Verdi's artistic aims. After many postponements, *Don Carlo* was premiered on March 11, 1867. While the reaction was mixed, Verdi himself did not hide the fact that he was disappointed in the results.

The original version of *Don Carlo* (the hero's name was subsequently italianized) had five acts. The Paris public, accustomed to the dramatic fireworks of earlier Verdi operas, failed to appreciate the grandeur of a score painted in darker, but much richer colors than any of his preceding works. The religious aspects of the plot offended some, including Empress Eugénie. Others criticized the Opéra for spending so much time and effort on a piece by a foreigner, especially since that piece turned out to be a curtain-raiser for the Paris International Exhibition of 1867.

After a few minor revisions and cuts made on the spot, Verdi reworked the entire score in 1883, condensing the five acts into four.

America heard *Don Carlo* for the first time at the New York Academy of Music in 1877. The Metropolitan Opera produced it in 1920 with a cast including Giovanni Martinelli, Rosa Ponselle, Margarete Matzenauer, and Giuseppe de Luca. Two years later, the role of King Philip II was sung by Feodor Chaliapine. In 1950, Rudolph Bing selected *Don Carlo* as the opening production of his reign as general manager. On that occasion, the title-role was sung by Jussi Bjoerling, and the new singers introduced in that performance included Fedora Barbieri, Cesare Siepi, and Delia Rigal. The conductor was Fritz Stiedry, and Margaret Webster made her debut as a stage-director at the Metropolitan Opera. On the West Coast, *Don Carlo* was given for the first time and in this translation by the Opera Theatre of the University of Southern California.

W.D.

THE STORY

ACT I. (Don Carlos, Crown Prince of Spain, has been betrothed to Elisabeth de Valois, daughter of Henry II of France, but learns that his own father, Philip II, claims her for his bride.)

Carlos seeks consolation at the cloister of the Monastery of St. Just, where the monks chant their prayers at the tomb of Charles V, Carlos' grandfather. His friend Rodrigo, Marquis of Posa, suggests that Carlos leave for the Netherlands, to cure himself of his infatuation and to protect the Flemish against the tyranny of Spain. The two men pledge friendship; King Philip and Queen Elisabeth approach the tomb, kneel briefly and proceed on their way.

In the cloister garden, Princess Eboli, the Countess of Aremberg and their ladies entertain themselves; Eboli sings a Moorish song to the accompaniment of Theobald's mandolin. As the Queen enters sadly from the monastery, Rodrigo appears, hands her a letter from Carlos and tells her that the Prince longs to see her. Elisabeth agrees to receive him, and the page leads Carlos to her side. The ladies retire. Carlos begs the Queen to obtain Philip's leave for him to go to Flanders and then declares his love in a passionate avowal. Breaking free of Carlos' embrace, Elisabeth turns him away. No sooner has he left than Philip reenters with his suite and, finding his wife unattended, banishes the Countess of Aremberg, who should have been at the Queen's side. Elisabeth consoles her; the ladies depart, leaving Rodrigo to plead the Flemish cause with Philip. The King suspects that Elisabeth and Carlos may have betrayed him and asks Rodrigo to watch the lovers, warning him of the Grand Inquisitor's enmity.

ACT II. At midnight Carlos awaits the Queen in her gardens in Madrid, following the instructions in a letter written, he believes, by Elisabeth but in reality penned by Eboli, who mistakenly thinks Carlos loves her. When the veiled Eboli enters, Carlos passionately declares his love; when she unveils, both realize their error. Furiously she accuses him of loving the Queen. Rodrigo comes upon them, grasps the situation and tries to placate Eboli, who runs from the garden swearing to expose Carlos and Elisabeth. To protect the Prince, Rodrigo takes certain incriminating papers from him.

In the square before the Cathedral of Our Lady of Atocha, in Madrid, an immense crowd awaits the appearance of King Philip. The monarch emerges from the church and is greeted by six Flemish deputies led by Carlos. Prince, populace and court plead for the King's mercy, but the friars insist on punishment for his rebellious subjects. Drawing his sword, Carlos swears to champion the Flemish cause in defiance of his father, who orders him disarmed. But Carlos surrenders his sword to Rodrigo, while all watch a group of heretics being burned at the stake.

ACT III. In his study Philip laments his wife's coldness. He then consults with the Inquisitor, who urges the death of both Carlos and Rodrigo. As the old man leaves, the King muses regretfully that the throne must always yield to the church. Elisabeth bursts in, crying that her jewel casket has been stolen. Philip hands it to her with an ironic demand that she open it. When she hesitates, he breaks the lock, revealing a portrait of Carlos, he accuses her of adultery. The Queen faints as Eboli and Rodrigo enter, the former confessing responsibility for Elisabeth's betrayal, the latter swearing to free Spain from political oppression. When the men have left, Eboli reveals to the Queen that she gave the casket to Philip from jealousy over Carlos' love and that she has been the King's mistress. Dooming Eboli to life in a convent, Elisabeth leaves her. The remorseful princess laments her fatal beauty and swears to save Carlos' life.

v

Rodrigo visits Carlos in prison and is shot to death by a minion of the Inquisition. The prince refuses to flee with Eboli but is given his liberty by his father as the furious mob storms into the cell to attack the monarch. Philip is protected by the Grand Inquisitor.

ACT IV. In the monastery cloister Elisabeth waits to bid farewell to Carlos. The lovers are surprised by Philip and the Grand Inquisitor, but Carlos is protected from them both when the ghostly Charles V emerges from the tomb and draws him into the shadows of the cloister.

Courtesy of Opera News

CAST OF CHARACTERS

PHILIP II, King of Spain	Bass
DON CARLO, Crown Prince of Spain	Tenor
RODRIGO, Marquis of Posa	Baritone
THE GRAND INQUISITOR	Bass
THE COUNT OF LERMA	Tenor
A FRIAR	Bass
ELIZABETH OF VALOIS, Wife of Philip II	Soprano
THE PRINCESS OF EBOLI	Mezzo-Soprano
THEOBALD, Elizabeth's Page	Soprano
THE COUNTESS OF AREMBERG	Mute
A ROYAL HERALD	Tenor
A CELESTIAL VOICE	Soprano

Flemish Deputies, Inquisitors, Gentlemen and Ladies of the Court of Spain, Pages, Guards of Philip II, Friars, Members of the Holy Office, Soldiers, Magistrates, Deputies from the Colonies of the Spanish Empire, etc.

TIME: Spain, about 1560

SYNOPSIS OF SCENES

			Page
ACT I	Scene 1	Cloister of the Monastery of St. Just	1
	Scene 2	The Garden adjoining the Monastery	29
ACT II	Scene 1	The Queen's Gardens in Madrid	101
	Scene 2	Square before the Cathedral	129
ACT III	Scene 1	The King's Study in Madrid	194
	Scene 2	The Prison of Don Carlo	243
ACT IV		Cloister of the Monastery of St. Just	271

DON CARLO

JOSEPH MERY and **CAMILLE DU LOCLE**
English Version by
WALTER DUCLOUX

Giuseppe Verdi

ACT ONE

PART ONE

The Cloister of the Monastery of St. Just. On the right a lighted chapel where we see, through a guilded gate, the tomb of Charles V. To the left a door leading outside into a garden with high cypress-trees. To the rear the entrance to the monastery proper. It is dawn.

(The monks are heard singing in the chapel.)

Copyright © 1958 by Walter Ducloux
Copyright assigned 1963 to G. Schirmer, Inc.

-to - re non è più che mu-ta ce - ner; del ce - le - ste suo fat -
splen - dor, Now re-turned to dust and ash - Charles the Fifth re - fused to
-to - -re non è più che mu-ta ce - -ner; del ce - le - ste suo fat -
- dor, Now re-turned to dust and ash - es, Charles the Fifth re - fused to
pp
pp
IL FRATE
Grandioso mf
Grand'è Dio sol, e s'Ei lo
Thine is the pow'r and Thine the
f
dim. ppp
-to - re l'al-ma al - te - ra or trema al pie'.
ren - der Un - to God his haugh-ty heart.
f
dim. ppp
-to - re l'al-ma al - te - ra or trema al pie'.
ren - der Un - to God his haugh-ty heart.
mf
F
dim.
vuo - le fa tremar la ter - ra ed il ciel!
glo - ry In Heav - en and on earth!
Ah!
Ah!
ff

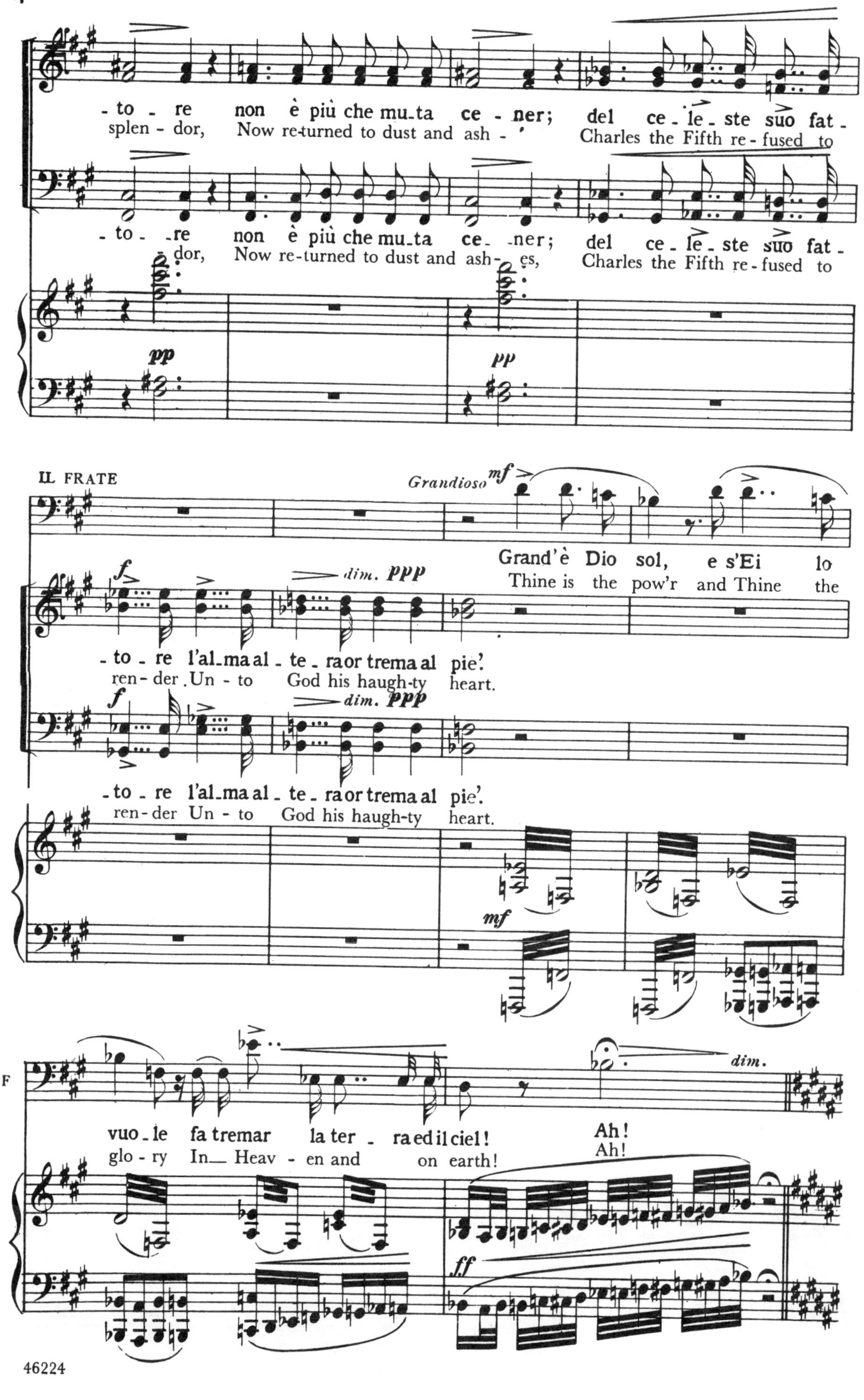

(The day dawns slowly, Don Carlos, pale and distraught, emerges from the vaults of the cloister. He stops to listen and uncovers his head. At the sound of a bell, the monks start leaving the chapel. They cross the stage and disperse in the cloister.)

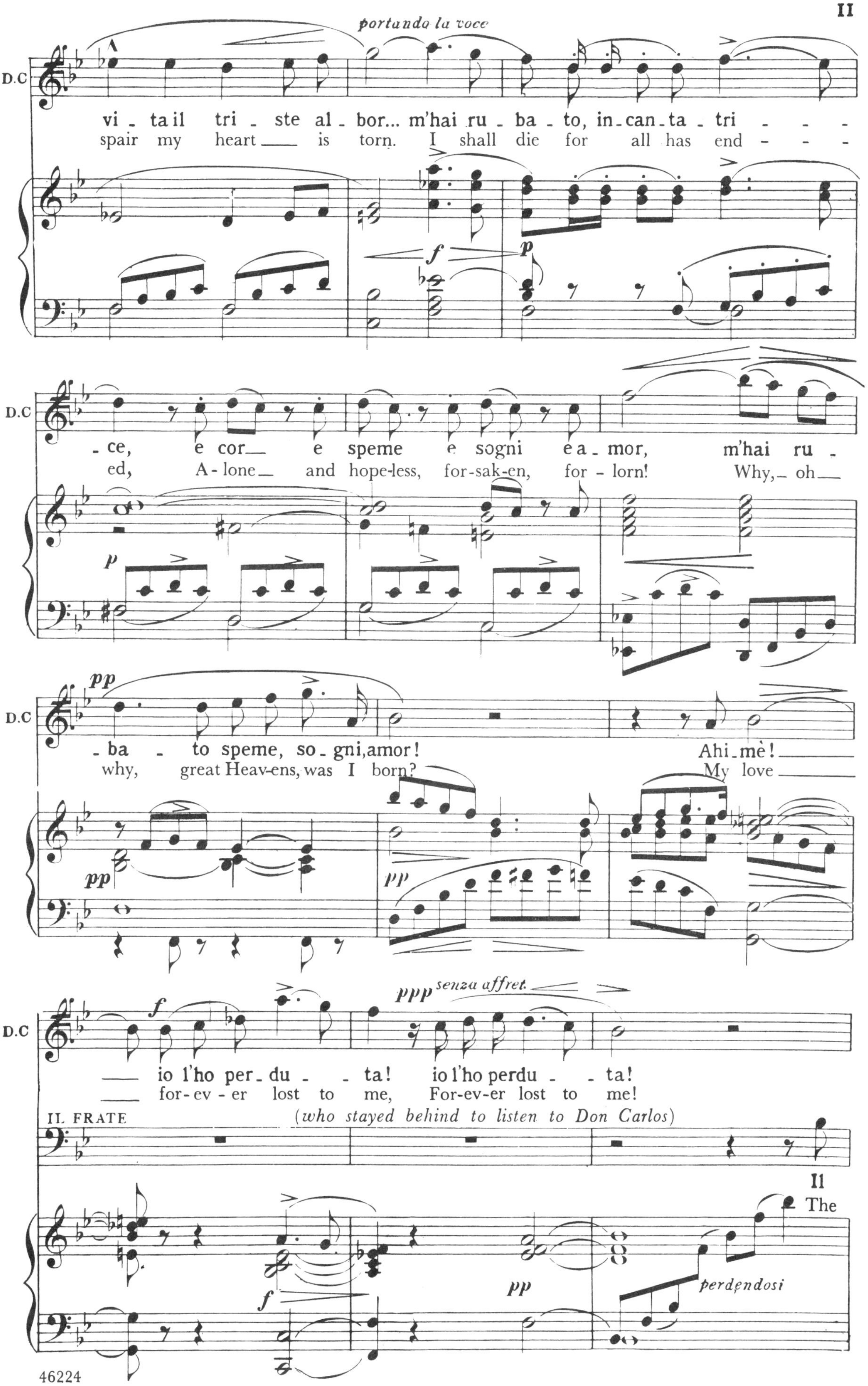
portando la voce
D.C
vi - ta il tri - ste al - bor... m'hai ru - ba - to, in - can - ta - tri - - -
spair my heart is torn. I shall die for all has end - - -
f
p
ce, e cor - e speme e sogni e a - mor, m'hai ru -
ed, A - lone and hope-less, for - sak - en, for - lorn! Why, - oh
pp
ba - to speme, so - gni, amor! Ahi - mè!
why, great Heav-ens, was I born? My love
f
ppp senza affret.
io l'ho per - du - ta! io l'ho perdu - ta!
for - ev - er lost to me, For - ev - er lost to me!
IL FRATE
(who stayed behind to listen to Don Carlos)
Il
The
perdendosi

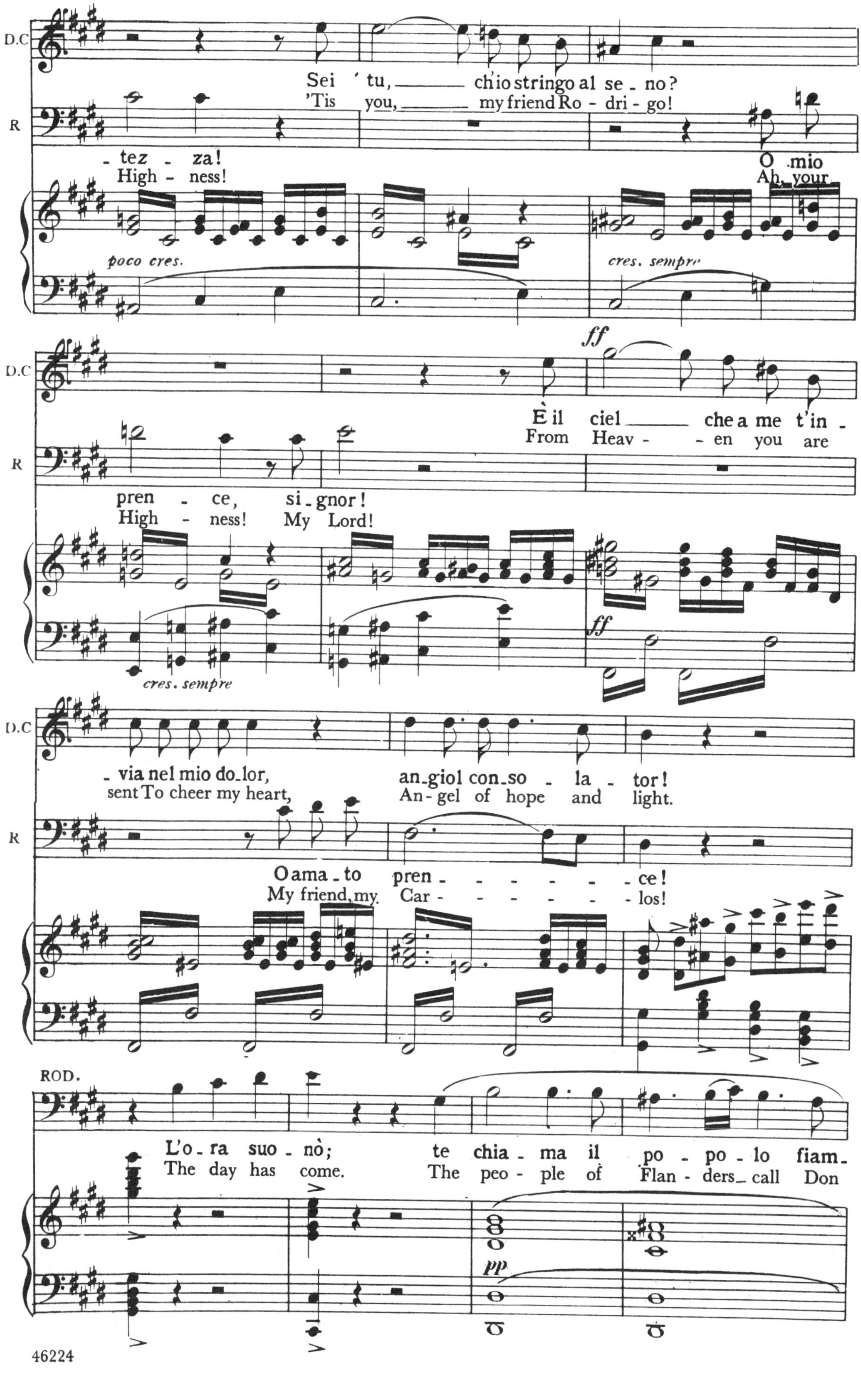

ACT ONE

PART TWO

In the garden adjoining the Monastery of St. Just. A fountain surrounded by grass-covered mounds and orange trees. On the horizon the blue mountains of Estremadura. Upstage right the door of the monastery.

(The Princess of Eboli, Theobald, the Countess of Aremberg and other ladies-in-waiting, pages, etc. The ladies are sitting on the grassy mounds around the fountain, pages at their feet. One of the pages is tuning a mandolin.)

UN POCO MENO
Sop. I.i e II.i
CHORUS
Sop. III.i
p
Sotto ai fol_ti, immen_si a_be_ti, che fan d'om_bre e di qui_
Gen-tle shad-ows so cool and ten-der Of these pines in their friend-ly
Sotto ai fol_ti, immen_si a_be_ti, che fan d'om_bre e di qui_
Gen-tle shad-ows so cool and ten-der Of these pines in their friend-ly
UN POCO MENO
_e_ _ti mi_te schermo al sa_cro o_stel, ri_pa_ria_mo e a noi ri_
splen - dor, Pi-ous guard-ians of bliss-ful calm, May you still our im-pa-tient
_e_ _ti mi_te schermo al sa_cro o_stel, ri_pa_ria_mo e a noi ri_
splen - dor, Pi-ous guard-ians of bliss-ful calm, May you still our im-pa-tient
sto _ri dien i rez_zi ai vi_vi ar_do_ri, che su
yearn - ing For re-lief from the sun-rays burn-ing, As we
sto _ri dien i rez_zi ai vi_vi ar_do_ri, che su
yearn - ing For re-lief from the sun-rays burn-ing, As we
A

no - i dardeggia il ciel, che su noi, che su
drink of your fra-grant balm, As we drink, as we
no - i dardeggia il ciel, che su noi, che su
drink of your fra-grant balm, As we drink, as we
no - i dar-deg-gia il ciel, che su no - - i, su
drink of your fra-grant balm. We are drink - ing, drink -
no - i dar-deg-gia il ciel, che su no - - i, su
drink of your fra-grant balm. We are drink - ing, drink -
poco rit.
(Theobald enters with Eboli)
noi, che-su-noi dar - deggia il ciel!
ing of your gen-tle fra - grant balm.
poco rit.
noi, che su noi dar - deggia il ciel!
ing of your gen-tle fra - grant balm.
B
leggero
poco rit.
a tempo
p

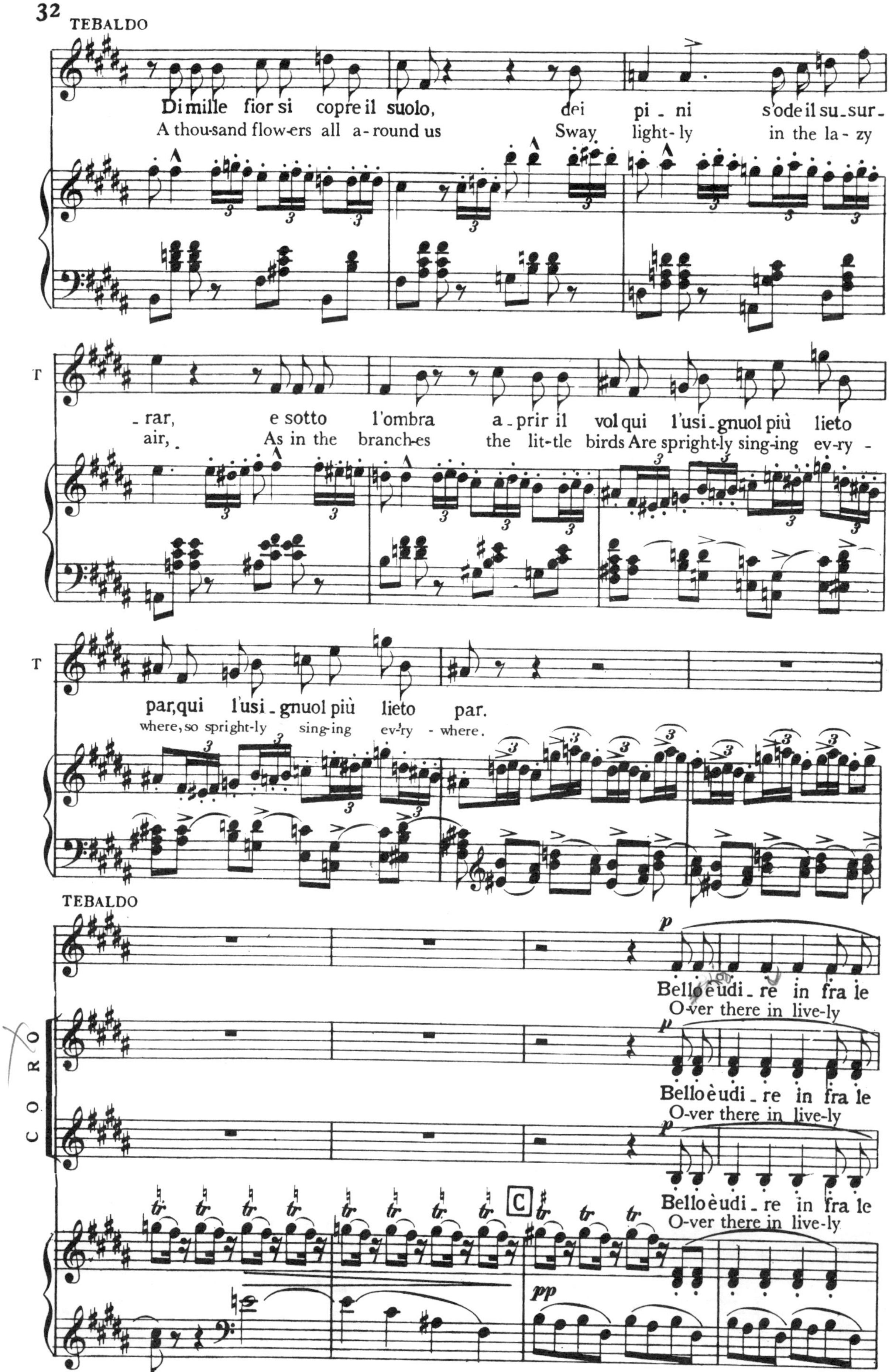

pian - te mormo - rar la fon - te a - man - te, stil - la a
danc - es, Whisp-ring pas - sion - ate ro - manc - es, Springs a

stil - la, i suoi do - lor! stil - la a stil - la, i suoi do -
foun - tain so clear and cool, Springs a foun - tain so clear and

- lor! E, se il so - le è più co -
cool. While the grove lends us pro -

T
cen - te, le o - re far del dì men
tec - tion, We can en - joy the sweet re -
cen - te, le o - re far del dì men
tec - tion, We can en - joy the sweet re -
cen - te, le o - re far del dì men
tec - tion, We can en - joy the sweet re -
T
len - te in - fra
flec - tion Of the
len - te in - fra
flec - tion Of the
len - te in - fra
flec - tion Of the
T
l'om - bra, in - fra l'om - bra e in mez - zo ai
blos - soms of the flow'rs in the silv - 'ry
l'om - bra, in - fra l'om - bra e in mez - zo ai
blos - soms of the flow'rs in the silv - 'ry
l'om - bra, in - fra l'om - bra e in mez - zo ai
blos - soms of the flow'rs in the silv - 'ry

roll the rs

pp
fior, in - fra l'om - bra ed i
pool, Of the blos - soms in the
fior, in - fra l'om - bra ed i
pool, Of the blos - soms in the
fior, in - fra l'om - bra ed i
pool. Of the blos - soms in the
poco rit.
fior, in fra l'om - bra e in mezzo ai
pool, Of the blos - soms in the silv'ry
fior, in - fra l'om - bra e in mezzo ai
pool, Of the blos - soms in the silv'ry
fior, in - fra l'om - bra e in mezzo ai
pool, Of the blos - soms in the silv'ry
dim.
poco rit.
I. Tempo
fior.
pool.
fior.
pool.
fior.
pool.
a tempo
E
mf

EBOLI
Tra queste mu_ra pi_e la Re_gi_ na di
Beyond these ho-ly por - tals In_sol-i-tar-y
pp
f
E
Spagna può sola pe_netrar. Vo_le_te voi, mie_com - pagne, già che le stelle in
wor-ship The Queen has gone to pray: Let us en - joy, while_ we are wait-ing, The ma - gic in the
E
ciel spun_ta_te ancor non son, can - - tar qual - che can -
air, And praise the flor-id boun - ty In mu - - sic and in
E
_zon?
song!
TEB.
Se_guir vo_gliam il tuo ca_
We are with you, We want to
CORO
Se_guir vo_gliam il tuo ca_
We are with you, We want to
Se_guir vo_gliam il tuo ca_
We are with you, We want to
F

37

(to Theobald)

38

(Eboli sings, accompanied by Theobald.)

♩. = 69
ALLEGRO BRILLANTE

EBOLI

Nei giardin del bel_lo sa _ racin o_stel_lo,
Night's en-chant-ing splen-dor Bade the world sur-ren-der,

al l'o_lez_zo, al rez_zo de_gli allôr, dei fior u _ na bel_l'al_
Si - lent fell the ven-dor, Still the streets be-low, As the Moor-ish

me _ a, tut _ ta chiu _ _ _ sa in vel, con _ templar pa _
beau - ty Kissed the moon _ _ so pale, Mind-ful of her

46224

E
pp
-re - a u - na stel - - - la in ciel. Mo - hammed, Re
du - ty, Through her silk - - - en veil. Came the King, - so
G
ff
p
p
moro, al giardin - sen va; di - cea lei: - t'a-
hand-some, So strong and tall: "What will be - your
pp
parlato
-doro, o gentil - bel - tà Vien, a sè t'in - vita per regna - re il
ran-som?" The King would call. "Come, my pret-ty maid-en, It is you I a-
H
Re; la Re-gi - na am-bi-ta non è più da me. Ah!
dore, For the Queen is fad-ing And a ter - ri - ble bore!" Ah!
3
3

E
Ah!
morendo
ah!
Ah!
Ah!
col canto
come un mormorio
sempre dim.
pp
Ah!
Ah!
ALL.º GIUSTO ♩=92
leggero
Tes_sete i ve_li,
Sly-ly in hid-ing,
TEBALDO
Ah! Tes_sete i ve_li,
Ah! Sly-ly in hid-ing,
ppp morendo
vaghe donzel-le, mentre è nei cie-li l'a_stro maggior,_ chè sono i ve-li,
nev-er con-fid-ing, Coy-ly de-cid-ing how much to show,_ Cau-tion be guid-ing
T
al_ brillar delle stel_le, più ca_ri all'amor.
firm-ly our heart, Till we show that we know where we go!

Accents strong

Sop. I.
Tes-sete i ve-li, va-ghe donzel-le, men-tre è nei cie-li l'astro maggior,
Sly-ly in hid-ing, nev-er con-fid-ing, Coy-ly de-cid-ing how much to show,

Sop. II.
Tes-sete i ve-li, va-ghe donzel-le, men-tre è nei cie-li l'astro maggior,
Sly-ly in hid-ing, nev-er con-fid-ing, Coy-ly de-cid-ing how much to show,

Sop. III.
Tes-sete i ve-li, va-ghe donzel-le, men-tre è nei cie-li l'astro maggior,
Sly-ly in hid-ing, nev-er con-fid-ing, Coy-ly de-cid-ing how much to show,

EBOLI
Al_____ bril-lar del-le stel-le, più ca-ri all'a-
Firm_____-ly our heart, Till we show that we know where we

TEBALDO
Al_____ bril-lar del-le stel-le, più ca-ri all'a-
Firm_____-ly our heart, Till we show that we know where we

chè sono i ve-li, al_____ bril-lar del-le stel-le, più ca-ri all'a-
Cau-tion be guid-ing firm_____-ly our heart, Till we show that we know where we

chè sono i ve-li, al_____ bril-lar del-le stel-le, più ca-ri all'a-
Cau-tion be guid-ing firm_____-ly our heart, Till we show that we know where we

chè sono i ve-li, al_____ bril-lar del-le stel-le, più ca-ri all'a-
Cau-tion be guid-ing firm_____-ly our heart, Till we show that we know where we

46224

I. TEMPO
E
-mor.
go!
T
-mor.
go!
-mor.
go!
-mor.
go!
-mor.
go!
ff
I. TEMPO
EBOLI
f
pp
Ma discer-no appe-na, (chia-ro il ciel non è)
"Let the moon be-hold you In his sil-ver-glow!
pp
E
mf
pp
i ca-pel-li bel-li, la man bre-ve, il piè
For my eyes have told-you That I love you so!

Deh! sol-le-va il ve-lo che t'a-scon- - - - -de a me;
Come, re-move the veil Which hides your face so fair,

es - ser co - me il cie - lo sen - za vel - - - tu dè.
You, whose charms so frail Cause e-ven stars to stare,

Se il tuo cor vorrai a me da-re in don, il mio tro-no a-
Let your heart be mine For the rest of my life! Make my nights di-

-vrai, chè so-vra-no io son = Tu lo vuoi? t'in-china, appagar ti
vine As my love-ly young wife!" "If you wish, come near-er! Your re-ward I

46224

44

vo'! = Al-lah! La Re-gi-na! Mohammed scla-mò. Ah!
bring." "Oh no! Al-lah help me! 'Tis the Queen!" said the King. Ah!

Ah! ah!
Ah! Ah!

come un mormorio   sempre dim.   *pp*

Ah!
Ah!

COME PRIMA

Tes-sete i ve-li, va-ghe donzel-le, mentre è nei cie-li l'a-stro maggior,—
Sly-ly in hid-ing, nev-er con-fid-ing, Coy-ly de-cid-ing how much to show,—

Tes-sete i ve-li, va-ghe donzel-le, mentre è nei cie-li l'a-stro maggior,—
Sly-ly in hid-ing, nev-er con-fid-ing, Coy-ly de-cid-ing how much to show,—

46224

E
chè sono i ve - li, al brillar del-le stel - le, più ca - ri all'a -
Cau - tion be guid - ing firm - - ly our heart, Till we show that we know where we
T
chè sono i ve - li, al brillar del-le stel - le, più ca - ri all'a -
Cau - tion be guid - ing firm - - ly our heart, Till we show that we know where we
E
- mor.
go!
T
- mor.
go!
CHORUS
Sop. I.
pp
Tes - sete i ve - li, va - ghe donzel - le,
Sly - ly in hid - ing, nev - er con-fid - ing,
Sop. II.
pp
Tes - sete i ve - li, va - ghe donzel - le,
Sly - ly in hid - ing, nev - er con-fid - ing,
Sop. III.
pp
Tes - sete i ve - li, va - ghe donzel - le,
Sly - ly in hid - ing, nev - er con-fid - ing,
M
p

E
T
Al brillar delle
Firm - - ly our heart, Till we
Remember
men-tre è nei cie-li l'a-stro maggior, chè sono i ve-li, al brillar delle
Coy - ly de-cid-ing how much to show, Cau-tion be guid-ing firm - - ly our heart, Till we
stel-le, più ca-ri all'a-mor.
show that we know where we go!
I. TEMPO
f
ff

47

48

EL. dì che lieto e_ra il mio cor!) / joy Will not re-turn a-gain.)

(Rodrigo appears in the background. Theobald approaches him. After a brief exchange of words, the page turns to the Queen to introduce Rodrigo.)

TEBALDO Il marche_se di Po_sa, Grande di Spagna. / Don Rod-ri-go de Po-sa, Gran-dee of Spain.

RODRIGO *(bowing to the Queen)* REC.^{vo}

A Si_gnora! Per Vostra Ma_e_ / My-la-dy, Her Maj-es-ty, the

(Rodrigo, while handing the letter to the Queen, quickly slips her a note, then shows the Ladies the royal crest on the letter. He whispers to the Queen.) *sotto voce e presto*

R _stà, l'augusta madre un foglio mi con_fi_dò in Pa_rigi. (Leggete, in nome della grazia e_ / Queen, your no-ble moth-er, Has asked me to bring you this from Pa-ris. (Read it, in the name of our Ho-ly

(in a normal voice)

(For a moment, Elizabeth remains motionless and confused while Rodrigo turns to Eboli.)

R _ter_na.) Ecco il re_gal sug_gel, i fior_da_li_si d'ôr. / Virgin!) The roy-al seal of France, A lil-y wrought in gold. **ALL^o. MODERATO**

B

49

EBOLI *(in a conversational tone, to Rodrigo)*

ALL⁰ ASSAI MOD.ᵗᵒ ♩=88

Che mai si fa nel suol france-se, co-sì gentil, co-sì cor-
And how is life a-cross the bor-der, In France, the home of law and

con eleganza

EB. -te-se?
ROD. or-der?

(to Eboli)

D'un gran tor-neo si par-la già, e del tor-
A tour-na-ment thrills ev-'ry heart. They say the

ELIS. *(holding the note in her hand)*

(Ah! non ar-disco
(I do not dare it,

-neo, e del torneo il Re sa-rà.
King him-self an-nounced He will take part.

p

(parlato)
EL.
aprirlo ancor;
se il fo, tradisco del Re l'o-
EBOLI (to Rodrigo)
to read it here!
How can I bear it, this dread-ful
Son le Francesi gen-ti - li tan - to, e d'e - leganza, di gra - zia han
And are the French-men as they claim to be, So strong and courteous, As all the Span-iards
EL.
- nor.
Ah! perchè tremo!
fear!)
(Heart, do not trem-ble!)
EB.
van - to.
(to Eboli)
ROD.
aim to be?
In voi bril-lar sol si ve-drà la
In you, in-deed, Na - ture has com-bined Both
EL.
Quest'alma è pu - ra, è pura anco - -
(to Rodrigo)
(My heart is blame - less, It still is blame
EB.
È mai ver ch'al-le fe-ste re-ga - li le Fran-
Is it true that at din-ners and danc-es, There in
R
gra - zia in-sie - me alla beltà.
beau - ty and bril-liance of the mind.
D

51

EL.
-sato a me caro, v'affi-date a costui, ven prego. Car-lo.)
gone but not for-got-ten, I be-seech you, to trust the bear-er... Car-los.")
EB.
se-ta e l'ôr sono e-le-gan-ti?
ROD. do they look? What are they wear-ing?
(to Eboli)
Tutto sta ben
How could I say?
(to Rodrigo)
Gra-ta io son. Un fa-
Thank you, Mar-quis! Do you
(with a bow to Eboli)
R
al-lor che s'ha la vo-stra grazia e la bel-tà.
All I can tell: I nev-er met a fair-er de-moi-selle!
F
p
-vor chie-de-te al-la Re-gi-na.
wish To ask the Queen a fa-vor?
(eagerly)
(aside)
(Io mi sostengo ap-
(God grant me strength to
Accet-to, e non per me.
I do, but not for me.

EL.
EBO. - pe_na!)
hear it!)
(to Rodrigo)
Chi più degno di voi può_ su_e bra - me ve_der_ ap_pa-
Not for you, Mar-quis? Who_then is wor - thy to seek a roy-al
(aside)
EL.
(Oh ter_ror!)
(Lord a - bove!)
EB.
-ga - te?
fa - vor?
f
EL.
Chi mai?
Yes, who?
EB.
Dite_lo, chi?
Who can it be?
ROD.
AND.te MOSSO ♩= 76
Cantabile
p
Car - lo ch'è sol il nostro a-
Car - los, your son, rest - less and
p
R
a tempo
-mo - re vi - ve nel duol su questo suol, e nessun sa quan_to do-
haunt-ed, He has come here in hope and fear. He, once so brave, strong and un-
a tempo

54

55

ANDANTE Come prima
EL.
EB.
ROD.
a tempo
Ah! Carlo del Re suo ge_ni_to_re rin_chiuso il
Ah! Carlos in vain sought from his fa - ther Guid - ance and
I
ANDANTE Come prima
a tempo
pp
a tempo
R
cor ognor trovò; ep_pur non so chi dell'a_
hope in his de-spair. Yet, in this world no-one should
a tempo
ppp
tr
a tempo
R
_mo - re sa - ria più de - gno, ah! inver nol so. Un sol, un
rath - er Proud - ly be loved as_a son and heir. One sin-gle
p col canto
J
a tempo
morendo
R
so_lo_det - to d'a_mo - re spa - rir il duo - lo_fa_rà dal
ges - ture of love and af-fec - tion Will ban-ish sor - row from Carlos'
col canto

57

EL.
gran Dio! Rive - derlo... è mo - rir!)
Oh God! To be near him is to die!)
EB.
per_chè lo ce - la, per_chè ce_lar - lo a me?)
Does Car - los love me? My heart's in hope and fear.)
R
- da, se
pain, Oh
ELIS.
R
tor - ne - rà, sal_vo sa - rà, se tor_ne_rà Car_lo fia sal -
help him find His smile a - gain! His smile a-gain! Car-los will smile a -
pp
f
(to Theobald, with dignity and firmness)
EL.
Va, pronta io son il figlio a ri - ve -
Go! I am pre-pared to see my
R
- vo.
gain!
p
a tempo
f
pp

59

Don Carlos is admitted by Theobald. Rodrigo quietly gives some instructions to Theobald who subsequently disappears into the monastery. Don Carlos slowly advances towards the Queen and bows to her without ever raising his eyes. Barely able to control her emotions, the Queen beckons him to come closer. Rodrigo and Eboli motion the ladies to disperse slowly among the trees. The Countess of Aremberg and two of the ladies stay nearby, somewhat unsure of what they should do. After a while they, too, pretending to gather flowers, withdraw gracefully.)

LARGO ♩ = 63 *(calmly)*

DON CARLO: Io vengo a domandar grazia alla mia Regina; quella che in cor del Re tiene il posto primiero sola potrà ottener questa grazia per me.

I come to beg the Queen For her gracious assistance, Knowing that of the heart of the King She is mistress. No-one could speak so well For my humble request.

ALL⁰ AGITATO ♩ = 80 *(increasingly excited)*

Quest'aura m'è fatale, m'opprime, mi tortura, come il pen-

A-round here I am dying,... Am choking... in frustration. Send me a-

61

(Absorbed in conversation, Rodrigo and Eboli cross the stage.)

Più Animato ♩= 80
riten.
♩= 88
Più Animato
D C
Ah! perchè mai parlar non sen - to nel vo - stro cor la pie - tà? Ahi -
Why in this fi - nal hour de - ny My yearn-ing for a sign of com - pas-sion? In -
p Più Animato ♩= 80
pp col canto
♩= 88
Più Animato
D.C
- mè! quest'alma è oppres - sa, ho in core, ho in core un gel In -
sane with suf-f'ring, and bro - ken, I need of your pit - y a to - ken! In
ff
D.C
- san! pian - si, pre - gai nel mio de - li - rio, mi vol - si a un
vain I want to die, to end the tor - ment, The sor - row, the
f
ELI.
ALL.º MODERATO ♩= 100
(greatly moved)
Perchè, perchè accusar il cor d'indif - fe -
But why, why blame my heart For cold-ness and in -
D.C
ge - - li do marmo d'a - vel!
an - guish: Which your cold heart de - fies.
B ALL.º MODERATO ♩= 100
pp

64

ren-za? Capir dovreste questo no— — bil si-len— —zio. Il do-
dif-f'rence,When you must know what bids My con- — -science be si- — -lent? Like a

-ver, co- me un rag- — gio al guar- do mio bril-
ray sent from Heav- -en My du-ty shines so

-lò; — gui-da ta-da quel rag- gio io mo-ve-
bright, — It guides my haunt-ed heart To what is

MENO MOSSO ♩=84

D.CAR.
-ro — La speme pongo in Dio, nell'inno-cen- -za! *(as if about to die)*
right, — and God on high Will help me try to find re-demp- -tion!

Perdu-to
Sink down, o

f *dolce espressivo*

46224

65

66

ciel pietà senti di tanto duol... I-sa-
last the angels take pity on my soul! Is-a-

Presto ad libitum (parlato)

Giusto ciel, la vita già
Oh Heaven, his life is in

(He faints.)

-bella, al tuo piè morir io vo' d'amor.
bel-la, my love,... oh joy to die with you!..

manca nell'occhio suo che lagrimò!
danger, His breaking eyes are filled with tears!

Bontà ce-
Oh, Holy

-leste, deh! tu rinfranca quel nobil core che sì pe-
Virgin, pray for him, Who suffers past endur-

parlante
E
-nò. Ahi-mè! il do-lor l'uc-ci-de... tra queste braccia io lo ve-
ing! His pain, his de-spair will kill him. And in these arms I shall en-
E
-drò morir d'affan-no, mo-rir d'a-mo-re... co-lui che il ciel mi de-sti-
fold, At last in ten-der em-brace to hold, The man whom God gave me to
MENO MOSSO ♩= 60
E
D.CAR. -nò! love!
(delirious)
Qual voce a me dal ciel scende a par-lar d'amor? E-li-sa-betta! tu, bell'ado-
A voice from Heav-en sent Came down to sing of love; My heart, to meet it, went Up to the
♩= 60
F MENO MOSSO
pp
E
O de-lirio, o terror!
I must lis-ten no more!
D.C
dolcissimo
-ra-ta, as-sisa accanto a me co-me ti vi-di un dì! Ah! il ciel s'il-
stars a-bove... En-tranced, my eyes can see A dream of mem-o-ry; 'Tis you, E-
pp

PIÙ ANIMATO
E
D.C
E_gli muo - - re! O ciel, ei muo - re!
He is rav - - - ing! May Heav-en save__ him!
- lu_minò, la sel_va ri_fio - rì!
liz - a-beth, My ra-diant bride-to - be.
cres.
O mio te -
Now you are
PIÙ ANIMATO
cres. sempre
gran Di_o!
May Heav-en...
cres.
- sor! sei tu, mio dol - ce a - mor! Sei
mine at last, Now you are mine at
allarg.
giu_sto ciel! Ah! giu - sto cie - lo! giu - sto
give me strength! Ah! Heav - en help_me! Gra - cious
tu! bel - l'a - do - ra_ta, bell'a - do - ra - ta,_sei tu,_ sei
last, Now you are mine yes, In all_ e - ter-ni-ty you are mine, are
f
secondando il canto

LO STESSO MOVIMENTO
E
ciel!
Lord!
parlante
(coming to)
D.C
tu!
mine!
Al_la mia tomba,
What am I say-ing?
al sonno dell'a_
Why bring me back to
G
LO STESSO MOVIMENTO
p
ALLEGRO ♩= 126
Oh! Carlo!
O Car-los!
_vel
life,
sottrarmi perchè vuoi, spieta_to ciel!
Now that I saw an end To pain and strife?
ALLEGRO ♩= 126
pp
oh! Carlo!
O Car-los!
pp
pp
D.CAR.
f
ALL.° AGITATO Più Sostenuto ♩= 120
Sotto al mio piè si di_schiuda la
O-pen the way to e-ter-nal dam-
ALL.° AGITATO Più Sostenuto ♩= 120
f
f

terra, il capo mio sia dal fulmin col-
nation! Death and decay may destroy all cre-

-pito, io t'amo, io t'amo, io
-ation! I love you, I love you, I

(taking her in his arms)
t'amo, Elisabetta, il mondo è a me sparito, sparito a
love you, Elizabeth, And if the world must end, I'll make you

ELI. PIÙ ANIMATO ♩= 138 (breaking free)
Compi l'opra, a svenar corri il padre, ed al-
Then go on to murder your father! With his

me!
mine!

PIÙ ANIMATO ♩= 138

E
-lor del suo san - gue macchia - to, ed al-lor del suo san - gue mac-
blood on your hands To the al - tar, With his blood on your hands, To ex-
mf
f
p
E
D.CAR. -chia - to all'al-tar puoi mena - re la ma - - - - - -
alt her, to em-brace as your wife Your own moth - - - - -
Ah!
Ah!
ff
mf
f
E
-dre, ed al-lor all'al-tar puoi mena - re la ma - - dre.. va.. va..
er . . . Yes, to lead to the al - tar, as wife, your own moth - er, go! Go!
mf
ff
E
D.CAR. va.. e sve-na tuo pa - - - - - - dre!
Go, and kill your fa - - - - - - ther!
(reeling back, aghast)
Ah! ma-le-det-to io
Al-might-y God! No!

(He flees in utmost despair.)
D.C
son!
No!
ff
I
p
ELI.
Ah! Id di - - - - o su noi
God the Lord, has saved Our hearts
pp
(She sinks to her knees.)
E
ve gliò! Si - gnor! Si -
once more! O Lord! O
p
E
- gnor!
Lord!
pp
morendo

King Philip, Theobald, the Countess of Aremberg, Rodrigo, Eboli, the ladies-in-waiting, Philip's entourage, and pages enter in quick succession.

ALL⁰ SOSTENUTO ♩= 126
(hurrying from the cloister)

TEBALDO: Il Re! / The King!

FILIPPO *(to Elizabeth)* Recit.:
Perchè sola è la Regina? Non una dama almeno presso di voi serbaste? Nota non v'è la legge mia regal? Quale dama d'o-
Why is the Queen alone? Not one among your retinue Attended to her duty? Do you not know what royal law demands? Of your ladies-in-

(The Countess of Aremberg steps out of the group and approaches the King, trembling.)
(to the Countess)
F
3
-nor esser dovea con voi?
Contessa, al nuovo
wait-ing, Who should have been with you?
My Count-ess, you re -
tr♭
f
p
p
(The Countess breaks out in tears.)
F
sol in Fran-cia tor-ne - re - te.
turn To France with-out de - lay!
ff
Soprani
(Everybody looks at the Queen, startled.)
pp
(Ah! La Re - gi - na e-gli of - fen - de!)
(Ah! 'Tis the Queen he has of - fend - ed.)
CHORUS
Tenori
pp
(Ah! La Re - gi - na e-gli of - fen - de!)
(Ah! 'Tis the Queen he has of - fend - ed.)
Bassi
pp
(Ah! La Re - gi - na e-gli of - fen - de!)
(Ah! 'Tis the Queen he has of - fend - ed.)
p

♩ = 50
ANDANTE ASSAI SOSTENUTO
p
pp
ELISABETTA
con espress.
Non pian - ger, mia com - pa - gna, non pianger
These tears of pain and griev - ing, Oh, stem their
pp
E
no, le - nisci il tuo do - lor. Ban - di - ta sei di
flow And dry their bit - ter dew! Though Spain you will be
E
p
dim.
B
Spa - gna ma non da - que - sto cor. Con
leav - ing, My heart will - stay - with you. To -

77

Ri - ce - vi e - stre - mo pe - gno, un pe-
Re - ceive of my af - fec - tion a to-

-gno di tutto il mio fa - vor; ce - la l'ol - trag - gio inde - gno on
-ken Which on-ly you shall wear! My sad - ness and de - jec - tion In

- de ar - ros - si - sco ancor. Non dir del pian - to
si - lence I shall bear. Con - ceal my grief and

mi - o, del cru - do mio do - lor; ri-
sor - row, My pain, this cruel mis - chance! Re-

- tor - na al suol na - ti - o, ti se - gui - rà il mio
turn - ing there to - mor - row, Oh greet the sky of

largo
E
cor, ah! ti segui_rà, ti segui_rà il mio
France, Ah, ah! The sun - ny sky of my be-lov - ed
f
p
dim.
cor. Ri_tor _ na al suol, al suol na_ti _ o,
France! Oh, greet up-on, up-on re-turn-ing,
RODRIGO
Spir_to gentil_e pi _ o acque _ ta il tuo do_lor, spir_to gen_til_e
Oh, may her no-ble heart To glad - ness be re-stored! Oh, may her no - ble
FILIPPO (aside)
(Come al cospet_to mio in_fin _ ge un no _ bil cor, come al cospet _ to
How in de-ceit-ful art To lie she can af-ford! How in de-ceit - ful
Sop.
Spir_to gentil_e pi _ o acque _ ta il tuo do_lor, spir_to gen_til_e
Oh, may her no-ble heart To glad - ness be re-stored! Oh, may her no - ble
Ten.
Spir_to gentil_e pi _ o acque _ ta il tuo do_lor, spir_to gen_til_e
Oh, may her no-ble heart To glad - ness be re-stored! Oh, may her no - ble
Bassi
Spir_to gentil e pi _ o acque _ ta il tuo do_lor, spir_to gen_til e
Oh, may her no-ble heart To glad - ness be re-stored! Oh, may her no - ble
CHORUS
E

80

ri_tor_na al suol, al suol na_ti_o,___ co_i vo_ti del cor, del___ mio
Oh, greet the sky of France to-mor-row, Greet the sky o-ver France, The___ sky of

pi_o acque_ta il tuo do_lor, il do_lor_____ il do_lor,
heart To glad-ness be re-stored! May her heart _____ be re-stored,

mio in_fin_ge un no_bil cor, in_fin_ge_____ in_fin_ge,
art To lie she can af-ford! How she lies! _____ How she lies!

pi_o acque_ta il tuo do_lor, il do_lor_____ il do_lor,
heart To glad-ness be re-stored! May her heart _____ be re-stored,

pi_o acque_ta il tuo do_lor, il do_lor_____ il do_lor,
heart To glad-ness be re-stored! May her heart _____ be re-stored,

pi_o acque_ta il tuo do_lor, il do_lor_____ il do_lor,
heart To glad-ness be re-stored! May her heart _____ be re-stored,

p

46224

(In tears, the Queen moves away from the Countess and leaves the scene, supported by Eboli. Everybody withdraws.)

♩= 96
ALLEGRO ASSAI MODERATO
(to Rodrigo)
(Rodrigo genuflects before the King, then goes towards him, without showing any sign of awe.)
FILIPPO
Re - state!
Re-main here!
pp
f
F
Presso alla mia perso - na perchè d'esser am -
I noticed you a-round me. Why have you nev-er
pp
p
- mes - so voi non chiede - ste an - cor?
yet En-deav-ored to speak to me?
A
Io so ri - compensar tutti i miei difen -
I know how to re-ward Those who fought for the
pp
p
RODRIGO
Spe - rar che mai po -
A du - ty well per -
- sor; voi ser - vi - ste, lo so, fido al - la mia co - ro - na.
crown. I know well what you did In the de-fense of Spain.
pp

R
-trei dal fa-vo-re dei Re? Si-re, pa-go son io, la — legge è scudo a
formed Needs no fur-ther re - ward. Sire, — I need no fa-vors. The law shall be my
R
me.
Lord.
FIL.
(after a pause)
Amo u-no spir-to al-tier. L'auda-cia per-do-no... non sempre...
You are a man of pride And seem in-de-pen-dent . . . be care-ful! . . .
PIÙ MOSSO
F
B
Voi la-sciaste il mestier della guerra; un uomo come voi, solda-to d'alta
PIÙ MOSSO
You have late-ly re-signed your com-mis-sion: How can a man like you, A sol-dier to the
p
ROD.
a tempo
O-ve al-la Spa-gna u-na spa - da bi-
Should once a - gain Spain have need — of her
F
stir-pe, i-ner-te può — re - star?
core, — En-joy a life — of rest?
a tempo
mf

R
-so-gni, u-na vin - di-ce man, un cu-sto - de all'o-nor, ben-to-sto
ser-vant, Of a man — who can fight, Of a pow - er-ful sword: Her glo-ry
— bril-le-rà la mia di sangue intri - sa!
FIL. — shall find My life at her com-mand at once.
C
Ben lo so... ma per voi — che far pos-
That I know. But for now — what are you
Nulla! No... nul-la per me! ma per altri
Noth-ing... no! Noth-ing for me, But for oth-ers...
F
-s'i-o? Che vuoi di-re? per
ask-ing? How sur-pris-ing... for
Io par-le-rò, Si-re, se gra-ve non v'è!
May I speak out, Sire? — Do I have your con-sent?
al-tri? Fa-vel-la!
oth-ers? Speak free-ly!

85

ROD. ALLEGRO ♩=116

O signor, di Fiandra arrivo, quel pa-
I have come, o Sire, from Flanders, From that
-e se un dì sì bel; d'ogni luce or fatto privo ispira or-
land once rich and fair; Yet to-day ev'rywhere one wanders The stench of

-ror, par muto avel! L'orfa nel che non ha lo co per le
death hangs in the air. Without food, naked and crying, Little

vie piangendo va; tutto struggon fer roe
orphans will bar your path, Swelling, with the scream of the

46224

fo - co, bandita è la pietà! La ri-
dy - ing, The roaring storm of wrath! From

piu animato

vie - ra che rosseggia scorrer sangue al guardo
farm and home come flying The hungry flames of

par; della madre il grido echeggia pei fi-
war, In vain a mother's sighing For

-gliuo - li che spirâr! Ah! sia
sons who are no more! Ah! I

PIÙ LENTO ♩= 80

be — ne—det — to Id — di — o, che nar—rar— lascia a
praise e—ter—nal— Heav—en For hav—ing brought me—

piu animato

me que—sta cru—da a—go—nia, perchè sia no — ta al Re, perchè sia no — ta al
here, Sire, To tell you the truth, No mat—ter how— se—vere, No mat—ter how— se—

♩= 92

Re.
vere.

FIL.

Col sangue sol po—tei la pa—ce a—ver del mon — do;
Ter—ror will of—ten serve To keep the world con—tent — ed.

il bran — do mio cal—cò l'or—goglio ai no—va—tor, che il lu — do—no le
In blood I had to drown Re—bel—lion on the rise, De—lud—ing people's

gen - ti coi sogni menti - tor'! La mor - te in questa man ha un av - venir fe - con -
minds With its fal-la-cies and lies. De-struc-tion, if wise-ly used, Is coun-ter-part to mer -

PIÙ MOSSO ♩ = 132

ROD.
Che! Voi pen - sa - te, se - mi - nan - do mor - te, pian -
Sire, do you hold That, if you sow de - struc - tion, You

- tar per gli anni e - ter - ni?
reap a bet - ter fu - ture?

Volgi un guardo alle Spa - gne! L'ar - ti -
Look a - round you and tell me: Is there

- gian cit - ta - din, la ple - be al - le cam - pa - gne a
one to com - plain? In Spain, with all her peo - ple, You

F
Dio fe-del e al Re un la-men - to non ha! La pace istessa io dono alle mie
find a hap-py land Un-der God and the crown. This is the kind of peace I want for
I
f
ROD.
con forza e molto presto
Orrenda, orrenda pa-ce! la pa-ce è dei se-polcri!
A peace of death and silence! Its sym-bol is the grave-yard!
F
Fian - dre!
Flan - ders.
J
ff
ff
(parlato a mezza voce, assai mosso)
Largo e ppp
lunga pausa
R
O Re! non abbia mai di voi l'istoria a dir: Ei fu Ne-ron!
O King, may nev-er His-to-ry once say of you: He was a Ne-ro!
dim.
ppp
ppp
ALLEGRO ♩ = 126
R
Quest'è la pa - ce
What you have brought, You
ALLEGRO ♩ = 126
mf

che voi da - te al mon - do?
claim to be sal - va - tion!

Desta tal don ter - ror, or - ror pro - fon - do! È un car -
What you have wrought in - stead Has been dam - na - tion! Sa - cred

- ne - - fi - ce il pre - te, un ban - di - to o - gni ar -
robes hide the hang-man, Hel - mets shield as - sas - sins'

- mier! Il po - pol geme e si spe - gne ta -
heads! The peo - ple trem-ble and suf - fer in

R
-cendo, è il vostro im-per de-serto immen - so, or-ren-do, s'ode ognun a Fi-
si-lence. Through-out this vast And seeth-ing reign of ter-ror Ev-ery mouth whis-pers
f
ff
Ped.
R
-lip-po ma-le-dir, sì, ma-le-dir!
curs-es A-gainst the King, yes, A-gainst the King!
R
N
Co - - - me un Dio
Like a god,
dim.
pp
R
re - - - den tor, l'or - - - be in-
heav- - - en sent, You could

molto dolce

ter, l'or be in ter rin no va te,
fash- -ion A world bright and splen- -dent,

ff

v'er ge te a vol, a vol su
Great- -er than all Who came be-

dim. *dim.*

bli- me, so vra d'o gn'al tro, d'o
fore you, Nev- -er to fade from the

pp

gn'al tro Re! Per voi, per voi
hearts of men: Through you a-rise

p *cres.*

R
f
— si al_lie_ti il mon _ do! da_te la li_ber_tà!
— The dawn of lib-er-ty! Oh, set your peo-ple free!
f
ff
mf
FIL.
Oh! strano so_gna
Dream-er so strange and
Q
F
_tor! Tu muterai pensier, se il cor dell'uom co_no_sce_
young! You could not speak like this If you would know the heart of
p
ppp dim. sempre
F
_rai, qual Fi_lip_po il co_no_ _sce!
man As Phil-ip has known it.
R
p

94

Or non più! ... Ha nulla inteso il Re...
But no more! ... The King has heard nothing!

Non temer! Sma ti guarda dal Grande Inquisitor!
Have no fear! But beware of the Grand Inquisitor!

ROD. Che! Sire!
Why!? Sire!

Tu resti in mia regal presenza e nulla ancora hai domandato al Re?
You have remained in the royal presence, And have not asked A favor of the King

Io voglio averti a me d'accanto!
I want to keep you near me from now on!

Sire! No! Quel ch'io son restar io vo'!
Sire, no! I should prefer To be what I am now!

Sei troppo alter!
You are too proud!

ALL.° MOD.to ♩= 100
sottovoce
F
O sò lo sguardo tuo pe - ne-trar il mio so-glio... Del ca-po mio, che grava
Although your search-ing eyes have seen The tri - als of my king-dom, You can not know the bit-ter
pp
la co-ro-na, l'an-go-scia ap-pren-di e il duol! Guarda or tu la mia
sor-row Rend-ing my heart and dis-turb-ing my soul. Cold and dark is my
poco allarg.
T
POCO PIÙ MOSSO ♩= 126
reggia! l'af-fanno... la cir-conda, sgra-zia - to ge-ni-tor! spo -
pal-ace, And haunt-ed by mis-for-tune... A wife whom I a-dore, Yet
con dolore
ROD.
Sire, che di-te mai?
Sire, what are you say-ing?
- so più tri-ste ancor!
whom I trust no more!
La Regi-na... un sospetto mi
The Queen... I am racked by sus-
ppp

(quickly)
R
Fiera ha l'alma insieme pu_ra! (breaking out in pain)
His_ heart is pure and no-ble!
F
tur_ba... mio fi_glio! Nul_la val sotto al
pi-cion . . . Don Car-los . . . What could ev - er re -
cres.
ciel il ben ch'ei tol_se a me!
place What Car-los stole from me?
(Rodrigo looks at the King in wordless apprehension.)
ANCORA PIÙ MOSSO ♩= 160
pp
U
Il lor de_
I shall en -
mf
ppp
_stin af_fi_do a te! Scru_ta quei cor, che un fol_le a_
trust their fate to you. Read in their hearts Now rent with
marcato
_mor tra_sci_na! Sempre le_cito è a te di scontrar la Re_gi_na!
heed-less pas-sion! You shall al-ways be free to en-coun-ter the Queen.
mf

a piena voce
f
F
Tu, che sol sei un uom, fra lo stuol u - man,
V
Vain - ly search - ing for one Since his reign be - gan,
pp
(aside, overwhelmed with joy)
ROD.
In-a-spet-ta
(Out of the night
allarg.
F
ri-pon-go il cor nel - la le-al tua man!
In you at last The King has found a man!
dolciss.
p
dolciss.
R
ta au - ro - ra in ciel ap - par!
a star so bright and fair
F
in tua man!
You a - lone!
Z
pp
pp stacc.

R
S'aprì quel cor quel cor che
Has filled with light His heart so
F
R
niun po-tè scru-tar!
full of dark de-spair!)
F
Pos-sa co-tan - - to dì la pa-ce a
Ah, could I know once more The peace of
mf
F
me tor-nar, pos-sa co-tan - - to dì la pa-ce a me tor-
mind of yore, Ah could de-scend once more the peace I knew be-
p
pp

LO STESSO MOVIMENTO ♩= 160
ROD.
In - a - spet - ta - - - - - - - - -
Out of the night,
F
- nar!
fore!
LO STESSO MOVIMENTO ♩= 160
R
♩= 160
LO STESSO MOVIMENTO
- ta au - ro - - ra in ciel ap - par!
o star so bright and fair!
F
Pos - sa tal
Y ♩= 160 Ah, could I
LO STESSO MOVIMENTO
R
Oh! sogno mio di - vin! Oh! sogno mio di - vin!
Of hope and light to dream! Of hope and light to dream!
F
dì la pace a me la pace a
know it, know it once more, peace shall de -
cres.

animando sempre
R
Oh! glo_ri_o _ sa spe_me!
O ray of hope and glo-ry!
F
pp
me tor _ nar!
scend once more.
Ti guar_da dal
Be-ware of the
ff
animando sempre
F
ppp
f
Grande Inqui _ si _ tor!
Grand In - - quis-i-tor!
Ti guarda!
Be care-ful!
Ti guar_da!
Be care-ful!
X
pp
f
ROD.
pp
(The King extends his hand to Rodrigo who kisses it while kneeling down.)
Si _ re!
Sire!
(The curtain falls quickly.)
pp
vuota
ff

ACT TWO

PART ONE

Prelude

102

A secluded grove with a fountain.
It is a clear night.

RECIT. (reading a note)

DON CARLO: «A mezza notte, ai giardin della Regina, sotto gli allòr della fonte vi-
"At mid-night, in the Gar-den of the Queen, near the ar-bor by the lit-tle

ALLEGRO

-ci-na». È mezza notte; mi par udir il mormorio del vicino
foun-tain." Mid-night has sound-ed. I seem to hear The gen-tle mur-mur of yon-der

ALLEGRO VIVO ♩ = 132

fon-te... Eb-bro d'a-mor,
foun-tain. Trem-ble, my heart,

eb-bro di gio-ia il core! E-lisa-betta! mio
rav-ing, In-sane with pas-sion! E-lizabeth, My

46224

ben! mio ben! mio tesor! a me vien!
love, my love, my de-light! Ah, come!

(Eboli enters, her face hidden by a veil.)

ALL⁰. AGITATO MOSSO ♩=144
(Don Carlos believes her to be the Queen and addresses her passionately.)

Sei tu, sei tu, bell'a_do_ra_ta, che ap-
'Tis you, yes, you, my love so ten-der Who

-pari in mezzo ai fior! sei tu, sei tu! l'al_ma be_
stands be-fore my eyes! 'Tis true, 'tis you! Your ra-diant

(sempre a mezza voce)

_a_ta già scorda il suo do_lor! O tu cagion del mio con_
splen__dor De-fies this cruel dis-guise. Oh, you who hold my heart un-

_ten_to, par_lar_ti posso al_men! o tu ca_gion del mio tor_
dy__ing, At last you heard my plea! Oh, you who cold-ly spurned my

EBOLI   (aside)

Un tanto a_mor è gioia a me su_
En-chant-ed mo-ment of pro-found e-

_mento, sei tu, a_mor mio, sei tu, mio ben!
cry-ing, Will now re_turn your heart to me!

PIÙ RITENUTO ♩=100

_prema. A__ma_ta, a_ma_ta io son!
mo-tion! Car_los loves me. His heart is mine!

con slancio

L'u_ni_ver__so obbli_
So for-ev___er fare

PIÙ RITENUTO ♩=100

46224

am! te sola, o cara, io bra — mo! Passato più non ho, non penso all'avve-
well, Farewell to tears and sorrow! Forgotten the world, Forgotten pain and

EBOLI
Pos - sa l'a-
Now that you

_nir! Io t'amo, io t'amo!
strife! I love you! I love you!

_mor il tuo cor al mio cor, il tuo cor sempre unir!
found me, may your passion surround me to the end of my life!

stringendo

L'universo obbli-
Like the stars in the

E
D.C
Oh! gio - ia su-pre -
I love - you for-ev -
- am, la vi-ta e il ciel i-stes - so! Io t'a - mo, io t'a -
sky My love shall last for-ev - er! I love - you for-ev -
8
♩=144 (She removes her veil.)
- ma!
er! (aghast, to himself)
Ahi-mè! Qual mai pen-
O Car-los! What sud-den
- mo!
er!
C
(Ciel! Non è la Re - gina!)
(God! It is not - the Queen!)
♩=144
ff
p
pp
- siero vi tien palli-do, im - moto, e fa gelido il labbro? Quale
no-tion has dis - turbed your mind? You tremble and your brow has turned pale.. Is it
(Carlos does not answer.)
allarg.
spet - tro si leva fra noi? Non credete al mio cor, che sol batte per voi? V'è i -
fear - that I may not be true? Are you doubt-ing my heart which beats only for you? You
ff
p
allarg.
col canto.

AND.te MOSSO ♩ = 69
(con passione)
E
-gnoto forse, ignoto an-co - ra qual fier agguato a'pie-di vo-stri sta? Sul
can-not know what all a - round you The e - vil forc-es of the Court have planned. Be-
AND.te MOSSO ♩ = 69
p
vostro capo ad ora, ad o - ra la fol-gore del ciel piombar potrà!
lov-ed, ev - er since I found you I fear for you, I fear their dead-ly hand.
D. CAR.
Deh!
I
D.C
nol credete: ad o-ra, ad o - ra più denso ve-do del-le nubi il vel; su
know the dan-gers that sur - round - me, the trait-ors who have made the prince their game, And
que-sto capo io veggo o - gno - ra pronta a scop-piar la fol - go-re del
all the forc-es that con - found - me May soon com - bine to end my life in

EBOLI
Udii dal pa_dre, da Posa i_stes_so in tuon sini _ stro di voi parlar. Sal_
I heard your fa - ther and your friend Po - sa in hateful words_discuss Don Carlos' heart. The
D.C
ciel!
shame.
Rodri_go!
Rod-ri -go!
E
_varvi poss'io, sal_varvi poss'io. I _ o v'a _ mo. Sal_varvi poss'io, sal_
one who can save you, See her in me, for I love you! The one who can save you,
Qual miste_ro a me si ri_ve_
What she tells_me_ Turns my heart to
(worried)
_varvi poss'io. Io v'a _ mo. Ah! Car _ lo!
See her in me, for I love you! Ah, Car - los!
_lò! qual miste _ ro! Il
stone, Turns my heart to stone. Your
D
pp
p

vostro in ver celeste è un co – re, ma chiu – so il mio restar
lov – ing heart is great and no – ble, But mine can – not take part

al gaudio dè! Noi facemmo ambe – due un – so – gno strano in notte
In joy – ful play. We were both in a dream, in a dream of enchantment, wrought by the

EBOLI
Un sogno! O ciel! Quelle parole ar-
Don Car – los! A dream! Those words of love and

sì – gentil, tra il profumo dei fior.
beau – ti – ful night And the spell of the moon.

– denti ad altra cre – deste rivolgere il – luso! Qual ba-
pas – sion were meant for an – oth – er... 'twas all a mis – take! Now I

III

E
R
E
- dè. (in a menacing tone) Tutto io so!
end! Now I know!
Chevuoi dir? Chevuoi dir? Sciagu - rata!
What do you mean? What do you mean, vi-cious vi-per?
L'intimo sei del Re I - gno - to non è a me.
You are the King's com- pan-ion. You see, I know you well.
Trema! io son...
Tremble! I am...
Ma una nemi - ca io son formi - da - bil, pos - sente: m'è no - to il tuo po -
I have no fear of you, For I, too, can be dan-g'rous. Your power I can as -
a piacere
col canto
- ter, il mio t'è i - gno - to ancor! Nulla!
ROD. sess, But you do not know mine. Noth-ing!
Che mai preten - di dir?
What do you mean by this?

ANDANTE SOSTENUTO ♩.=58
(with subdued but unmistakable meaning, to Rodrigo)
E
Al mio fu-ror sfuggite inva-no, il suo de-stin è in questa
My wom-an's heart you have of-fend-ed. On-ly re-venge will ev-er
ANDANTE SOSTENUTO ♩.=58
p
mano.
ROD. mend it.
(to Eboli)
Parlar do-ve-te, a noi sve-la te qual mai pensie-ro vi trasse
I want to know what brought you here, What e-vil mis-chance Has made you ap-
Io son la ti-gre al cor, al cor fe-ri-ta, al-la ven-det-ta l'offe-sa in-
Just like the tig-ress, wound-ed, wild and bleeding, will tear her foes be-fore re-
R
qui.
pear!

E
-vi-ta.
ced-ing.
R
Su voi del ciel cadrà il fu-ror. Degli innocen-ti è il protet-
Let God the course of jus-tice chart! Heav-en a-lone can read our
E
Il mio fu-ror sfuggite in-va - - - - - - no,
D. CARLO
My wom-an's heart you have of-fend - - - - - - ed.
Stol-to fui! stol-to
Through my fol - - - - - - ly, my
R
-tor. Su voi del
heart. Let God the
ff
E
è il suo de-stin in questa ma - - - - - no.
On-ly re-venge will ev-er mend it.
D.C.
fui! Oh de-stin spie - -
fol - - - - - ly, My rav - - - - ing
R
ciel ca-drà il fu-
course of right - - - - eous-ness

115

Il mio furor sfuggite inva - no, è il suo destin in questa ma - no.
My woman's heart you have offend - ed, On-ly re-venge will ev-er mend it.

-ta - to! d'u-na ma - - - - dre ho il nome mac-
mad - ness, I have turned my de-light in-to

-ror: de - gli in - no - cen - ti è il pro - tet -
chart! For Heav-en a-lone can read our

Ah! voi m'a - ve - te in cor fe -
Ah! like a ti - gress, wound - ed and

-chia - to! Sol Id - dio in da-gar po-
sad - ness! On - ly He who guides the stars on

-tor.
heart.

Parlar dove te, a noi svela - te
I want to know what e-vil de - mon,

-ri - - ta, al - - la tear
bleed - - ing, will tear

-trà se
high, He may

qual mai pensier vi trasse qui, qual mai pen_
I want to know what brought you here, I want to

E
D.C
R
ven - det_ta l'offe - - sa in_vita, ah voi m'ave_te nel cor fe_ri - - -
a - part_ her foes re - ced-ing, like - a - ti-gress, so wild and bleed - -
que - sto cor colpa non ha. Sol Id - -
save our souls un-til we die! On - ly
_sier, qual mai pensier vi tras_se qui. Su voi del
know what brought you here, what brought you here. Let God a -
espress.
_ta, al_la ven_det_ta l'offesa in vi - ta, il mio fu_ro - re
ing, will tear a-part_ her foes re - ced - ing. Ah my deep-est pas - sion
_di - - o in_dagar_ po_trà se_que_sto
He who guides the stars_on high, May_He_pro -
ciel, su voi_ ca - drà il fu_ror: degli inno_cen - ti,
lone the course of right - eous - ness chart! For He in Heav - en,
sfug - - gi - te in va - - - - - - -
you have of - fend - - - - - -
co - - - re col - pa non
tect us un - til we
de - gli in_no - cen - - ti è il pro - tet -
Yes, He a - lone can read our

E
D.C
R
G
_no, al mio fu_ror sfuggite inva_no, il suo destin è in questa
ed. My wom-an's heart you have of-fend-ed. On-ly re-venge will ev-er
ha.
die! p
tor; su voi del ciel cadrà il fu
heart. Yes, He a-lone can read in our
ma_no, il suo de_stin è in questa ma_no, nel cor m'ave _ te fe_
mend it. On-ly re-venge will ev-er mend it. Be-cause you scorn my deep-est
Oh de - - - stin, oh de -
Through my fol - - - - ly, my
_ror: de - - gl'in - - - no - - -
heart. Let Him the
dim.
_ri_ta, al mio fu_ror sfuggi_te invan, al mio fu_ror sfuggi_te in_
pas-sion You try in vain to flee my wrath. My wom-an's heart you have of -
_stin spie - - - ta - to!
rav - dim. - ing mad - ness,
_cen - ti è il pro - tet - tor, su voi del ciel
course of jus - tice chart! Yes, He a-lone

E
-va-no, il suo de-stin è in questa mano, il suo destin è in questa
fend-ed. On-ly re-venge will ev-er mend it, On-ly re-venge will ev-er
D.C
ho d'u - na
I turned de -
R
cadrà il furor; de - - -
can read in our heart. Let
E
ma-no, nel cor m'ave - te fe-ri-ta, al mio fu-ror sfuggi-te in-
mend it. Be-cause you scorn my deep-est pas-sion, You try in vain to flee my
D.C
ma - - - dre mac-chia - - - to l'o -
light in - to sad - - - ness and
R
-gli in - - - no - - - cen - ti è il pro - tet -
Him the course of jus - tice
E
-van, voi m'ave-te in cor, in cor fe -
wrath. Like a ti-gress will tear her foes a -
D.C
-nor! sol Id - dio in-da-gar po -
fright! On - ly He, guid-ing the stars on
R
-tor, su voi del ciel ca-drà il fu-
chart! May He guide us and read in our

E
D.C
R
-ri-ta, voi m'ave-te in cor, nel cor fe-
part! So my bit-ter de-spair Will strike your
-trà se que-sto cor, se questo cor col-pa non
high May save our heart, May save our heart Un-til we
-ror; de-gl'in-no-cen - - - ti e gli è il pro-tet-
heart, Yes, He a-lone, He can read in our
-ri-ta, il mio fu-ror, il mio fu-ror
heart, Your e-vil heart, Your e-vil heart
ha, se que-sto cor col-pa non
die, Un-til we die, Un-til we
-tor, il pro-tet-tor, il pro-tet-
heart, Read in our heart, Read in our
pp
su di voi piombe-rà
I shall tear it a-part.
ha.
die!
-tor.
heart.
f
ff

120

_len an_co_ra non stil_lò quel labbro male_detto!   Ro_drigo, frena il
snake that must be killed at once Before spilling its poison!   Not

EBOLI
Perchè tardi a fe_rir?   Non indugiar an_cor!   Perchè tardi?
What is staying your hand?   Kill me and make an end!   What prevents you?

cor!
that!

No.   No.
No.   No.

ROD. *(throwing the dagger away)*
No, u_na spe_me mi re_sta; m'i_spi_rerà il Si_gnor.
One single hope I have left now. The Lord will give me strength.

col canto

ALL⁰ AGITATO
EBOLI *(to Don Carlos)*
Trema per te, fal_so fi_gliuo_lo, la mia ven_detta ar_ri_va
Dread and dis-may shall strike with hor-ror In-to your heart their blinding

ALL⁰ AGITATO

46224

E
già. Trema per te, fra poco il suo - lo sotto il tuo piè si schiu - de -
flash! When my re - venge I have to - mor - row, Vile and cor - rupt, your world will
♩= 138
rà!
crash.
D.CAR.
Tutt'ella sa!
It is too late!
ROD.
Tacer tu dêi; ri - spet - ta il duo - lo, o un Dio se -
Do not be - tray his bit - ter sor - row, Or you shall
pp
Trema!
Trem-ble,
trema!
trem-ble!
D.C
tutt'ella sa!
It is too late!
R
- ve - ro ti pu - ni - rà. Tacer tu dêi, o per te il
rue your deed too rash! Do not be - tray him, or to

E
D.C
R
tremar tu dêi, tremar
Ah, you shall pay, in fear
tremendo duolo!
Des-per-ate sor-row!
op - pres - - so il
My heart is
suo - - - lo sotto il tuo piè si schiude - rà, sì tacer tu
mor - - - row O-ver your head the world will crash! Yes, Do not be -
tu dêi, tremar tu dêi!
to pay, de-spair to pay!
cor, for - za non ha: tut - to ella sa, tut - to ella
lost, my will is gone! All now is use-less, all now is
dêi, sì tacer tu dêi, o per te il suol si schiude -
tray him, or you will pay, O - ver your head the world will

E
D.C
R
Tremaper te, fal-so fi-
Dread and despair shall strike with
sa!—
vain!—
Tutt'ella sa! tre-men-do
It is too late, Oh, end-less
-rà, o-per te il—suo-lo si schiude-rà.
crash, Or—o-ver—you—the—world will crash!
Tacer tu dêi; ri-spetta il
Do not be-tray his bit-ter
p
mf
-gliuo-lo, la mia ven-detta ar-ri-va già.
hor-ror In-to your heart their blinding flash!
Tremaper te, fra po-co il
When my re-venge I have to-
duo-lo! oppresso il cor for-za non ha.
sor-row! My heart is lost, my will is gone!
Tutto ella sa! nè anco-ra il
It is too late, for by to-
duo-lo, o un Dio se-ver ti pu-ni-rà.
sor-row, Or you will rue your deed so rash!
Ta-cer tu dè, o per te il
Do not be-tray him, or to-

PIÙ MOSSO
E
suo - lo sotto il tuo piè si__schiu - de rà! Tremar, tre_mar, tremar tu
mor - row, Vile and cor - rupt, your__world__ will crash. In wild de - spair and fear you'll
D.C
suo - lo sotto il mio piè si__schiu - de rà! Ah! que_sto suo - lo, questo
mor - row Crumbling to dust, my__world__ will crash. Ah, end - less sor - row, end -less
R
suo - lo sotto il tuo piè si__schiu - de - rà! Tacer tu dè, o per te il
mor - row, O - ver your head the__world will crash! Do not be - tray him, or you'll
PIÙ MOSSO
ff
E
dêi,__ tre_mar__ tu dêi, tremar tu dè, fra poco il suo_lo, fra po - co il
pay,__ in fear__ you'll pay! For my re-venge will start to-mor-row, to - mor-row you'll
D.C
suo_lo si schiu - de - rà, ah que_sto suo_lo, questo suo_lo si schiu - de -
sor-row, The world__ will crash. My heart is lost, my will is gone! For the world__ will
R
suo_lo si schiu - de - rà, tacer tu dè, tacer tu dè,__ ah! tre_ma che il
pay_for your deed__ so rash! Do not be - tray him, Or you'll pay__ to - mor-row For

(exits in wild fury)
E
suol sotto il tuo piè si schiu_de_rà_ sot _ t'al tuo piè!
pay, And then the world a-round will die — in — fi - nal crash!
D.C.
_rà, or que_sto suol si schiu_de_rà_ sot _ t'al mio piè!
crash. Ah, yes, the world a-round will die — in — fi - nal crash!
R
suo_lo sot _ t'il tuo — piè si schiu _ de_rà!
our world a - round will — die in fi - nal crash!
L
ROD.
Carlo! se mai su te fogli importan_ti
Car-los, if you have on you cer-tain notes and
R
serbi, qualche no_ta, un se_gre_to, a me affi_dar_li
pa-pers of im - por-tance, may-be se-cret... En-trust them to my
D.CARLO
(hesitating)
POCO MENO MOSSO
A te! all'intimo del Re!..
To you, the king's most trusted friend?
R
dêi. So_spet_ti tu di me? di
care! Have you lost faith in me, in
POCO MENO MOSSO
col canto

A TEMPO PIÙ VIVO ♩=126
D.C
R
No, no, del mio cor sei la spe-
No, no! You a-lone in all Cre-
me? di me? sospetti di me?
me? Are you sus-pi-cious of me?
M
p
-ranza: questo cor che sì t'a-mò a te chiu-de-re non
a-tion, You a-lone can know the woe Of this heart that loves you
so. In te ri-po-si ogni fi-dan-za:
so. My friend, my on-ly way to sal-va-tion!
sì, questi fogli impor-tanti ti do!
ROD. Here, take my let-ters and pa-pers in trust!
Car-lo, tu
Car-los, I

Io m'abban_do _ no a te,   m'abbando _ no a te.
I hand my life to you,   hand my life to you!

puoi,   tu puoi fi _ da _ re in me,   puoi fi_dar_ in me.
vow,   I vow my life to you,   vow my life to you!

(They fall into each other's arms.)

ACT TWO

PART TWO

A vast square in front of the Cathedral of Our Lady of Atocha. To the right, the church, with an impressive flight of steps leading up to it. To the left, a palace. To the rear, another flight of steps seems to lead to a lower square in the center of which a stake has been erected whose top can be seen. The horizon is formed by large buildings and distant hills.

(The sound of festive bells is heard. A milling crowd, held in check with difficulty by halberdiers, fills the stage.)

(A funeral march is heard. A group of monks is crossing the stage, leading those condemned by the Inquisition.)

CHORUS OF PEOPLE

Soprani I.
Spunta to ecco il dì d'e sul tan za, o
Re-joic - ing to-day in this roy - al display, We

Soprani II.
Spunta to ecco il dì d'e sul tan za, o
Re-joic - ing to-day in this roy - al display, We

Tenori
Spunta to ecco il dì d'e sul tan za, o
Re-joic - ing to-day in this roy - al display, We

Bassi
Spunta to ecco il dì d'e sul tan za, o
Re-joic - ing to-day in this roy - al display, We

131

-stra - - - - to, il mon - do è pro - stra - - to al suo
name shall re-sound and his fame be re-nowned To the end of Cre -
-stra - - - - to, il mon - do è pro - stra - - to al suo
name and his fame be re-nowned To the end of Cre -
-stra - - - - to, il mon - do è pro - stra - - to al suo
name shall re-sound and his fame be re-nowned To the end of Cre -
-stra - - - - to, il mon - do è pro - stra - - to al suo
name shall re-sound and his fame be re-nowned To the end of Cre -
marcato
piè! Il nostro a -
a - tion! Love and de -
piè! Il no - - stro a -
a - tion! Love and de-vo - - tion to
piè! Il nostro a - mor o - vun - que l'accompagna,
a - tion! Love and de - vo - tion fol - low him al - ways,
piè! Il no - stro a - mor o - vun - que, o - - -
a - tion! Love and de-vo - - tion fol - - low him. He
B
pp
m.d.

-mor o-vun - que l'accompa - - - gna, e que - sto a - - -
vo - tion fol-low him al - - - ways, Yes, our de - - -
-mor, il nostro a-mor o - vun - que l'accom-
him, fol - - low him al - - - ways, and shall nev-er
e questo amor e
Nev - - - er our love, nev - - -
-vun - que l'ac - - - com - pa - - - gna, e que - - - sto a-
guides us right through day and dark - - - est
-mor giammai, giammai non sce - me-
vo - tion! The sky on high can see our
-pa - - gna, e questo amor giammai, giam-
die Nev - - - er shall die, Our love for
questo a-mor giam - - mai non sce - - - me - -
- - er our love shall die, no nev - - - er
-mor giam-mai giammai non sce - - - - me-
night. The sky on high can see our

No breath
-rà, giam-mai, giam-mai. Il
love, the sky on high. May
-mai non sce-me-rà, no Il
him shall nev-er die! No! May
-rà, giammai sce-me-rà, no Il
die, it shall nev-er die! Ah! May
-rà, non sce-me-rà. Il
love shall nev-er die! May
tr
no-me suo, il no-me suo è l'or-
long live his reign, To the glo-ry of Spain, Yes, the
no-me suo, il no-me suo è l'or-
long live his reign, To the glo-ry of Spain, Yes, the
no-me suo, il no-me suo è l'or-
long live his reign, To the glo-ry of Spain, Yes, the
no-me suo, il no-me suo è l'or-
long live his reign, To the glo-ry of Spain, Yes, the
f
8

Practise words.

(si ode una marcia funebre)

-go - -glio_del_la Spagna, e vi_ver deve nell'e_terni_tà.
Glo - ry__ of Spain__ and the grandeur and majesty of our illustri-ous na - tion!

-go - -glio del_la Spagna, e vi_ver deve nell'e_terni_tà.
Glo - -ry of Spain and the majesty of our il-lus-tri-ous na - tion!

-go - -glio_del_la Spagna, e vi_ver deve nell'e_terni_tà.
Glo - ry of Spain__ and the grandeur and majesty of our il-lus-trious na - tion!

-go - -glio_del_la Spagna, e vi_ver deve nell'e_terni_tà.
Glo - ry of Spain__ and the grandeur and majesty of our il-lus-tri-ous na - tion!

C *pp sottovoce e stacc.*

46224

CORO DI FRATI *(The monks cross the stage, leading the condemned towards the stake.)*

Il dì, il dì spuntò, di del terrore,
il dì tremendo, il dì feral. Morran,
morran, morran! giusto è il rigore,
giusto gli è il rigor dell'Im- mor-

The day, the day has come, the day of terror,
The day of judgment, the day of death. To die,
to die, to die behooves the sinner.
Just and great is the will of the Im-

137

_tal._____
mor - - tal.

D *Cantabile espressivo*

Ma di per - dón voce su-
But in the end a voice from

-pre - ma all'a-na-te-ma succe - - derà, se il peccator
Heav-en Will lift the ban from the soul of those Who will re-nounce

all'ora estre - ma, all'ora estre - ma si pen - ti-
in true re-pen-tance Their e-vil thoughts of sin and re-

46224

138

139

al più gran - - de dei Re
glo - - ry and fame to the King.
- rà. Vi - - - - - -
die! Our
Il suo no - - me è l'or -
Long live his reign, To the
- go - glio di Spa - - - - gna, e vi -
Spain, to her glo - - - - ry, To the
del - la Spa - gna, e vi - vrà nel - - - - l'e -
to the splen - dor of Spain in e -
f
p
cresc.

O—nor al
Oh glo—ry

vrà nel l'e—ter—ni—tà
fer—vor shall nev—er die

go—glio di Spa—gna, e vi—vrà nel l'eter—ni-
glo—ry of Spain and her fame in e—ter—ni-

vrà e vi—vrà nel l'eter—ni-
glo—ry of Spain in e—ter—ni-

ter—ni—tà, vi—vrà nell'e—ter—ni-
ter—ni—ty! May long live our glo—ri-ous

Vi—vrà nell'e—ter—ni-
May long live our glo—ri-ous

142

Re, o-nor al Re, o-nor al
be, Long live the King! Glory to

O-nor al Re, o-nor al
Long live the King! Glory to

-tà. O-nor al Re, o-nor a
ty! Long live the King! Glory to

-tà. O-nor al Re, o-nor al
ty! Long live the King! Glory to

-tà. O-nor al Re, o-nor al
King! Long live the King! Glory to

-tà. O-nor al Re, o-nor al
King! Long live the King! Glory to

46224

Re, o-nor al Re, o-nor al Re!
him! Long live the King! Glory to him!

Re, o-nor al Re, o-nor al Re!
him! Long live the King! Glory to him!

Re, o-nor al Re, o-nor al Re!
him! Long live the King! Glory to him!

Re, o-nor al Re, o-nor al Re!
him! Long live the King! Glory to him!

Re, o-nor al Re, o-nor al Re!
him! Long live the King! Glory to him!

Re, o-nor al Re, o-nor al Re!
him! Long live the King! Glory to him!

Re, o-nor al Re, o-nor al Re!
him! Long live the King! Glory to him!

(Rodrigo, the Count of Lerma, Elizabeth, Theobald, pages, ladies-in-waiting, gentlemen of the realm, and heralds now enter in a solemn procession from the palace. All the state offices, the court, the imperial deputies from the Spanish provinces, are represented. The procession comes to a halt in front of the church steps.)

145

146

CUT TO P54

H
pp
cresc.
Sop. I.
Sop. II.
Ten.
Bassi
CHORUS OF PEOPLE
f
Spun-
Re-
I
riten.

I° TEMPO
ta - - to ecco il dì d'e - sul - tan - - - za, o -
joic - - ing to - day in this roy - al dis - play, We
ta - - to ecco il dì d'e - sul - tan - - za, o -
joic - - ing to - day in this roy - al dis - play, We
I° TEMPO
ff
no - re, o - nore al più grande dei Re - - - gi! In
hon - or King Phil - ip in grate - ful pros - tra - - - tion. We
nor al più gran - - de dei Re - - gi! In
hon - or the King in pros - tra - - - tion. We

es - so hanno i po - - pol fi - dan - - za, il mon - - do è pro -
pledge him our faith, and that loy - - al we stay, As his
es - so hanno i po - - pol fi - dan - - za, il mon - - do è pro -
pledge him our faith, and that loy - - al we stay, As his
es - - so hanno i po - - pol fi - dan - - za, il mon - - do è pro -
pledge him our faith, and that loy - - al we stay, As his
es - - so hanno i po - - pol fi - dan - - za, il mon - - do è pro -
pledge him our faith, and that loy - - al we stay, As his
-stra - - - to, il mon - do è pro - stra - to al suo
name shall re-sound and his fame be re-nowned To the end of the
-stra - - - to, il mon - do è prostra - to al suo
name and his fame shall re-sound To the end of the
-stra - - - to, il mon - do è pro - stra - to al suo
name shall re-sound and his fame be re-nowned To the end of the
-stra - - - to, il mon - - do è pro - stra - - to al suo
name shall re-sound and his fame be re-nowned To the end of the

PIÙ ANIMATO ♩=120

piè! — Onor al
world! — Long live the

piè! — Onor al
world! — Long live the

piè! — Onor al
world! — Long live the

piè! — Onor al
world! — Long live the

J **PIÙ ANIMATO** ♩=120

p

Re! — Onor al
King! — Long live the

Re! — Onor al
King! — Long live the

Re! — Onor al
King! — Long live the

Re! — Onor al
King! — Long live the

Re! King!
Re! King!
Re! King! O-nor! The King!
Re! King! O-nor! The King!
O-nor al Re! vi - - - -
Long live the King, long
O-nor al Re! vi - - - -
Long live the King, long
Ei vi - - - -
The King! Long
Ei vi - - - -
The King! Long
ff

-vrà nel - - - l'e - - - ter - - - ni - - - tà,
may he live, long live his
-vrà nel - - - l'e - - - ter - - - ni - - - tà,
may he live, long live his
-vrà nel - - - l'e - - - ter - - - ni - - - tà,
may he live, long live his
-vrà nel - - - l'e - - - ter - - - ni - - - tà,
may he live, long live his
ei vi - - - vrà nel - - - l'e - - - ter - ni - -
glo - rious reign, For - - - ev - er live his
ei vi - - - vrà nel - - - l'e - - - ter - ni - -
glo - rious reign, For - - - ev - er live his
ei vi - - - vrà nel - - - l'e - - - ter - ni - -
glo - rious reign, For - - - ev - er live his
ei vi - - - vrà nel - - - l'e - - - ter - ni - -
glo - rious reign, For - - - ev - er live his

ff
-tà, ei vi - - - vrà
reign, Long may he live
nel - l'e - ter - ni - tà, ei vi - - -
In e - ter - ni - - ty! Long may he

-vrà nel-l'e-ter-ni-tà. Onor al
live in e-ter-ni-ty! Long live the
Re! Onor al Re!
King! Long live the King!
cresc.

ANDANTE SOST.º ♩= 69
(A Herald addresses himself to the portals of the church which are still closed. Everyone bears his head.)
L'ARALDO REALE
Schiusa or sia la por_ta del tem_pio! O ma_gion del Signor, t'apri o_mai! Sa_cra_rio ve_ne_ra_to, a no_i ren_di il no_stro Re!
O-pen wide, you por-tals of mer-cy, O-pen wide, ho-ly house of the Lord! O sa-cred Shrine of Faith, Give to his peo-ple their King!
ANDANTE SOST.º ♩= 69
CHORUS OF PEOPLE
Sop. I e II.
Sop. III.
Ten.
Bassi
Schiusa or sia la por_ta del tem_pio! O ma_gion del Signor, t'apri o_
O-pen wide, you por-tals of mer-cy, O-pen wide, ho-ly house of the

156

_mai!___ Sa_cra_rio ve_ne_ra_to, a noi ren_di il nostro Re!
Lord!___ O sa-cred Shrine of Faith, Give to his peo-ple our___ King!

(When the church portals open, we see King Philip in full regalia, the golden crown on his head, surrounded by monks. The people kneel down. The grandees cover their heads.)

ALL⁰. ASSAI SOST⁰ ♩ = 84

46224

157

FILIPPO

Recit.
Nel posar sul mio capo la corona, popol', giurai al ciel, che me la dona, dar morte ai rei col fuoco e con l'acciar.
When I first placed the crown upon my head, my people, I swore to God whose grace had crowned me, To root out evil By fire and by sword.

Maestoso ♩=72

(Everyone bows in silence.)

CHORUS OF PEOPLE

Sop. I e II.
Gloria a Filippo! Gloria al ciel!
Praise be King Philip! Praise be God!

Sop. III.
Gloria a Filippo! Gloria al ciel!
Praise be King Philip! Praise be God!

Ten.
Gloria a Filippo! Gloria al ciel!
Praise be King Philip! Praise be God!

Bassi
Gloria a Filippo! Gloria al ciel!
Praise be King Philip! Praise be God!

46224

(Philip descends the stairs and takes the Queen's hand in order to continue the procession.)
ALL.º MOSSO ♩ = 138
morendo
N
ELISABET.
(All at once, six Flemish deputies, clad in brown, appear, led by Don Carlos. They kneel at the King's feet.)
(aside) (Qui Carlo! O ciel!)
(Don Car-los! 'Tis he!)
RODRIGO
(aside) (Qual pensier lo so-spinge!)
(What has moved him to come here?)
D.CARLO
Son messag-ger' del Brabante e di Fiandra ch'il tuo figliuol ad-du-ce innanzi al
They have been sent From Bra-bant and Flan-ders, And your own son has brought them To see the
R
FILIPPO
Chi son co-stor prostrati innanzi a me?
Who are these men Be-fore me on their knees?
D.C

AND^te ASSAI MOSSO
♩ = 76
D.C
Re.
King.
cantabile con molta espress.
6 DEPUTATI
Si - re, Si - re, no, l'o - ra e - strema anco - ra non suo -
Sire, Sire! Sor - row and grief have brought us here, o
AND^te ASSAI MOSSO
0 ♩ = 76
cantabile espress.
p stacc.
6 D
- nò per i Fiammin - ghi in duol. Tut - t'un po - po - lo t'im -
Lord, To speak for Flan - - - ders. Steeped in tears, the Flem-ish
6 D
- plo - ra, fa che in pian - to co - sì sempre non ge - - ma.
peo-ple look to you in their plea For right-ful mer - - - cy.
pp
pp
6 D
Se pie - to - so il tuo co - - re la clemen - za e la
Heav - - en's glo - ry has crowned you: Let its mer - cy sur -

160

pa_ce chie_dea nel tem_pio, pie-
round you And fill your heart with peace! O

_tà di noi ti pren_da, di noi pie_tà, pie_tà ti
Sire, grant us your pit-y in our dis-tress, Show us com-

pren_da, e sal_va il no_stro suol, e sal_va il no_stro
pas-sion, And spare our be-lov-ed land! Oh, spare the soil of

FILIPPO

A Dio voi fo_ste in
The God whom you of -

suolo, o Re,_che avesti il tuo poter da Di___o.
Flanders, King,_whom God Him-self lent might and Hon - -or!

161

ELISABETTA
TEBALDO
D. CARLO
RODRIGO
F
6 FRATI
Sop. I.
Sop. II e III.
Ten. I.
Ten. II.
Bassi
CORO DI POPOLO
Q
pp
riten.
f
p
Su di lor stenda il Re la sua ma_no so_
May the King in his heart grant them grace and com-
me.
way!
A
The
Ah! son___ co_stor_ in_ fi_di,
The_Lord___ they have_of_fend_ed,
in
The

a tempo
riten.
F
-vrana,
pas-sion!
tro-vi pie-tà, signor, il Fiammingo nel
May they find mer-cy, Lord, In their bit-ter de-
T
D.C
R
Dio voi fo-ste in-fi-di, in-
God whom you of-fend-ed? The
6 F
Dio, in Dio non han la fe', in
ho-ly faith they have be-trayed. The
p

a tempo
riten.
E
duol,
spair!
tro - vi pie - tà, signor, il Fiammingo nel
May they find mer - cy, Lord, in their pain and de -
T
D.C
R
F
- fi - - di al vo - - stro Re.
King whom you be - - tray?
6 F
Dio, in Dio non han la fe'.
ho - ly - faith they have be - trayed.

a tempo
E
duol, pie - tà, si
spair! O Lord, no
T
duol, pie - tà! nel suo mar - tir
spair! O Lord, oh end their grief,
D.C
duol, pie - tà, si
spair! O Lord, no
R
duol, pie-
spair! O
F
Lun-gi da me, lun-gi da me, a Dio fo - ste
Out of my sight, out of my sight, You who fos - ter
6 F
Vede te in
Their e - vil
a tempo
duol, pie - tà! nel suo mar - tir
spair! O Lord, oh end their grief,
duol, pie - tà! nel suo mar - tir
spair! O Lord, oh end their grief,
duol,
spair!
duol, pie - tà! nel suo mar - tir
spair! O Lord, oh end their grief,
duol, si - gnor, pie -
spair! O Lord, have
a tempo

E
T
D.C
R
F
F
-gnor, pie - tà, si - - - -
more of strife and
pres - so a mo - rir ei man - - da già
Bring them re - - lief! Oh, hear them sigh!
-gnor, pie - tà, si - - - -
more of strife and
-tà, si - - gnor, pie - tà, pie -
Lord, no more of war! O
in - fe - de - - - li, al Re - fo - - ste
strife and trea - - - son, you who fos - - ter
lor sol dei ri - bel - li, ve - de - te in
heart up - holds re - - bel - lion. Their e - vil
pres - so a mo - rir ei man - - da già
Bring them re - - lief! Oh, hear them sigh!
pres - so a mo - - rir ei man - - da - già
Bring them re - - lief! Oh, hear them sigh!
pie - - - - tà, si - - - -
O Lord, no
pres - so a mo - rir ei man - - da già
Bring them re - - lief! Oh, hear them sigh!
tà, pie - - - - tà, del Fiam - -
mer - - - cy, no more of

E
T
D.C
R
F
6 F
-gnor, pie - tà! nel suo mar - tir
war! Bring Flan-ders' shore re - lief!
l'e - stre - mo so - spir nel suo mar -
They must not die. Oh, end their
-gnor, pie - tà! nel suo mar - tir
war! Bring Flan-ders' shore re - lief!
-tà, si - gnor, pie - tà! nel suo mar -
Lord, no more of war! Bring them re -
in - fe - de - li: va - dan lontan, lontan da
strife and trea - son. Out - of my sight, take them a -
lor sol dei - ri - belli! Tutto il rigor mertan del
heart up-holds re - bel-lion. Their bold up-ris - ing must be
l'e - stre - mo so - spir pie - tà, si -
They must not die. O Lord, no
l'e - stre - mo so - spir pie - tà, si -
They must not die. O Lord, no
-gnor, pie - tà, pie - tà,
more of war! O Lord,
l'e - stre - mo so - spir pie - tà,
They must not die. O Lord,
-min - go in duol pie - tà, si -
strife and war, no more of
cres.

E
T
D.C
R
F
6 F
__ pres_so a ______ mo _ rir ahi! __ man _ da già, ei man _ da
__ And_ end ______ her _ grief! Ah, __ hear them sigh! They must not
_tir, nel suo mar _ _ _ tir, presso a mo _ _ rir, ei manda
grief, Bring them re _ _ _ lief! Ah, hear them sigh! They must not
__ pres_so a ______ mo _ rir ______ ei man _ _ _ _ da già
__ And_ end ______ her_ grief! ______ They must not die.
_tir, nel suo mar _ _ _ tir, presso a mo _ _ rir, ei manda
- lief! Oh, end their grief Ah, hear them sigh! They must not
me, va_dan lontan, lon_tan da me.
way! Out_of my sight, take them a - way!
Re, tutto il rigor mertan del Re!
crushed. Their bold up-ris - ing must be crushed.
_gnor, pie _ _ tà, si _ _ _ gnor.
more of strife and war!
_gnor, pie _ _ tà, si _ _ _ gnor.
more of strife and war!
— o si _ _ _ gnor.
no more war!
— o si _ _ _ gnor.
— no more war!
_gnor, pie _ _ tà, si _ _ _ gnor.
war, oh no more war!

169

170

cres.
E
— nel — suo — mar - tir, — pres - so a — mo - rir, —
— Bring — them — re - lief! — O — Lord, — no — more —
T
— nel — suo — mar - tir, — pres - so a — mo - rir, —
— Bring — them — re - lief! — O — Lord, — no — more —
D.C
— nel — suo — mar - tir, — pres - so a — mo - rir, —
— Bring — them — re - lief! — O — Lord, — no — more —
R
nel
And
F
so - - - - - - no i Fiam - minghi a me ri -
These Flemish - traitors who have fos - - - - tered re -
6 D
- plo - ra, fa che in pian - to co - sì — sempre non
peo - ple look to you in their plea — For right-ful
6 F
in Dio non han, non han la —
Our ho - ly faith they have be -
— nel — suo — mar - tir, — pres - so a — mo - rir, —
— Bring — them — re - lief! — O — Lord, — no — more —
pie - - tà, si - -
No more of
pie - - tà, si - -
No more of
pel Fiammin - go nel duol, pie -
end their pain and de - spair! No

172

sempre cresc.
ff
l'e - stre - mo sospir, ah! pie - tà, si -
They must not die. Ah, have mer - cy, o
l'e - stre - mo sospir, ah! pie - tà, si -
They must not die. Ah, have mer - cy, o
l'e - stre - mo sospir, ah! pie - tà, si -
They must not die. Ah have mer - cy, o
già l'estremo sospir, ah! pie - tà, si - gnor, si -
sigh - ing! They must not die. Ah, my Lord, they must not
in - fe - de - li a Dio, al Re, a Dio, al
are be - tray - ing both God and King, both God and
pren - da e sal - va il no - stro suol, o Re, che avesti il tuo poter da Di -
land! Oh, spare the soil of Flanders, King, whom God himself lent might and hon -
lor sol dei ri - bel - li, tutto il ri - gor mertan del
heart up holds re - bel - lion. Their bold up - ris - ing must be
sempre cres.
l'e - stre - mo sospir, ah! pie - tà, si -
They must not die, Ah, have mer - cy,
del Fiam - min - go in duol, pie - tà, ah! pie - tà, si -
y on Flan - ders, Lord, and grant, grant them your mer - cy,
del Fiam - min - go in duol, pie - tà, ah! pie - tà, si -
y on Flan - ders, Lord, and grant them your mer - cy,
tà, si - gnor, pie - ta - de, o si -
war! O Lord, have mer - cy, o
sempre cres.
ff
E
T
D.C
R
F
6 D
6 F

Un poco animato
cres.
E
-gnor, tro--vi pie--tà tro--vi pie--tà, pie--tà, si--
Lord! Oh, may they find your heart in--clined to grant them
T
-gnor, pie-tà, si--gnor, pie--
Lord! Be kind, o Lord, and
D.C
-gnor, pie--tà, si--gnor, pie--tà, si--
Lord! Be kind, o Lord, Be kind, o
R
-gnor, tro--vi pie--tà, tro--vi pie--tà, pie--tà, si--
die. Oh, may they find your heart in--clined to grant them
F
Re!
King!
6 D
-o!
or!
6 F
Re!
crushed.
-gnor!
Lord!
-gnor!
Lord!
-gnor!
Lord!
-gnor!
Lord!
S
Un poco animato
cres.

E
f
pp
-gnor, del Fiam - min - - go che
mer - - - - - cy in their grief and de- -
T
pp
-tà del Fiam - min - - go che muor, che
grant them your mer - - - cy in their de - - -
D.C
pp
-gnor, del Fiam - min - go, del Fiam - min - - go che.
Lord, end their grief and end their bit - - - ter de- -
R
pp
-gnor, del Fiam - min - - go che
mer - - - - cy in their grief and de-
F
6 D
ff
Pie-
O
6 F
pp

E
muor, pie - tà, pie - tà, pie -
spair. Oh, may they find your
T
muor, pie - tà, si - gnor, pie - tà, si - gnor, pie - tà, si -
spair. Oh, may they find your heart in - clined to grant them
D.C
muor, pie - tà, si - gnor, pie - tà, si - gnor, pie - tà, si -
spair. Oh, may they find your heart in - clined to grant them
R
muor, pie - tà, si - gnor, pie -
spair. Oh, may they find your
F
a Dio, a Dio voi fo - ste in - fe - de - li, in - fe -
The law of God you have of - fend - ed, King and Crown and
6 D
- tà di noi ti pren - da, pie - tà di noi ti
spare the soil of Flan - ders, Oh, spare the soil of
6 F
a Dio, a Dio voi fo - ste in - fe - de - li, in - fe -
The law of God you have of - fend - ed, King and Crown and
S.1i
ah! pie - tà, si - gnor, pie - tà, si - gnor, pie - tà, si -
Lord! Oh, may they find your heart in - clined to grant them
S.2i 3i
pie - tà, si - gnor, pie - tà, si - gnor, pie - tà, si -
Ah, may they find your heart in - clined to grant them
T.1i
pie - tà, si - gnor, pie - tà, si - gnor, pie - tà, si -
Ah, may they find your heart in - clined to grant them
T.2i
pie - tà, si - gnor, pie - tà, si - gnor, pie - tà, si -
Ah, may they find your heart in - clined to grant them
B.
ah! pie - tà, si - gnor, pie - tà, si - gnor, pie - tà, si -
Lord! Oh, may they find your heart in - clined to grant them
f
ff

E
T
D.C
R
F
6 D
6 F
pp
f
tà pie - tà del Fiam - min - - - go - che
heart in - - - clined to grant them mer - - - cy, o
gnor pie - - tà del Fiam - min - - - go - che
mer - - - cy, Lord, grant them mer - - - cy, o
gnor pie - - tà del Fiam - min - - - go - che
mer - - - - cy, Lord, grant them mer - - - cy, my
tà pie - - tà del Fiam - min - - go nel
heart in - - clined to grant them mer - - - cy, my
de - - li al vo - stro Re, al vo - stro Re, a
ho - ly faith you have be - - trayed, you have be - trayed. Yes,
pren - - da, e sal - - va e sal - va il no - - stro
Flan - - ders, have pit - - - y on, pit - y on our
de - - li al vo - stro Re, al vo - - - - stro
ho - ly faith you have be - - trayed, you have be - -
gnor pie - - tà del Fiam - min - - go - che
mer - - - - - cy, Lord, grant them mer - - - cy, o
gnor pie - - tà del Fiam - min - - go che
mer - - - - - cy, Lord, grant them mer - - - cy, o
gnor pie - - tà del Fiam - min - - go che
mer - - - - cy, Lord, grant them mer - - - cy, o
gnor pie - - tà del Fiam - min - - go che
mer - - - - - cy, Lord, grant them mer - - - cy, o
gnor pie - - tà del Fiam - min - - go che
mer - - - - cy, Lord, grant them mer - - - cy, o

E
muor, ab - - - - bi pie -
Lord! Mer - - - - - cy, o
T
muor, pie - - - tà, si -
Lord! Be kind, o
D.C
muor, ab - - - - bi pie -
Lord! Mer - - - - - cy, o
R
duol, pie - - - tà, si -
Lord! Be kind, o
F
Dio voi fo - ste in - fi - di, in -
God you have of - - - fend - ed, The
6 D
suol, ah! pie - tà, pie -
souls. Ah, oh, spare our
6 F
Re, son co - stor dei ri - bel - li,
trayed. In their hearts they bear re - bel - lion.
muor, ab - - - - bi pie -
Lord! Mer - - - - - cy, o
muor, si - - - gnor, pie -
Lord! Be kind, o
muor, si - - - - gnor, pie -
Lord! Mer - - - - cy, o
muor, si - - - gnor, pie -
Lord! Be kind, o
muor, si - - - gnor, pie - -
Lord! Be kind, o

179

E
ff
-tà,
Lord!
ab - - -
Ah,
T
-gnor,
Lord!
D.C
ff
-tà,
Lord!
ab - - - - -
Ah,
R
-gnor,
Lord!
F
lon-tan— va— dan da me,—lon - tan-da— me,
Go, lead these trai - tors a-way! Go, lead these trai - tors a - way!
6 D
ff
-tà,
land,
ah sal - - va,
Ah, spare — our
6 F
sì tut-to, tut-to il ri-gor—mer - - tan-del— Re,
Their bold re-bel-lion must be crushed, it must be crushed without de-lay!
-tà,
Lord!
-tà,
Lord!
-tà,
Lord!
-tà,
Lord!
-tà,
Lord!
f

E
- - bi pie-tà, si - gnor!
bring them peace, o Lord!
T
si - - - - gnor!
O Lord!
D.C
- - bi pie-tà, si - gnor!
bring them peace, o Lord!
R
si - - - - gnor!
O Lord!
F
vadan lontan da me!
Out of my sight, a-way!
6 D
salva il nostro suol, o Re!
Flan-ders, spare our na - - - tive land!
6 F
in fi - - - - di!
The trai - - - - tors!
si - - - - gnor!
O Lord!
si - - - - gnor!
O Lord!
si - - - - gnor!
O Lord!
si - - - - gnor!
O Lord!
si - - - - gnor!
O Lord!
p
f

182

ALLEGRO ♩.=104

D. CARLO

Si — re! egli è 'tempo ch'io vi — — — va. Stanco
Sire! — I shall hide it no long — — — er: I am

son — di se — guir una e — sis — ten — za o — scura, in questo
wea — — ry of lead — — ing An ex — is — tence of lei — sure Here at your

suol! Se Dio vuol — che il tuo
court. If one day, — by the

ser — to que — sta mia fron — te un
will of God, — Your — man — — tle

46224

giorno a cinger venga,
shall fall On my shoulders,

per la Spagna prepara un Re degno di lei!
It is time you prepare me For crown and royal duty.

FILIPPO
Il Brabante e la Fiandra a me tu dona.
To command over Flanders You shall name me!

Insensato! chieder tanto ardisci!
It is madness to request such a favor!

Tu vuoi ch'io stesso porga a
You wish that I should hand you The

184

te l'ac- ciar che un dì immo-le-reb- be il
sword which you, one day, Will turn a- gainst the

D.CAR.
Ah! Dio legge a noi nei cor; Ei giu-di-
Ah! God can read my heart. He a-lone will

Re!
King.

ELISABETTA
Io tre- mo!
I trem-ble!

(drawing his sword)
Io qui lo giu- ro al
So help me God! I

-car ci de'.
judge us all.

Ei si per- dè!
He went too far!

ciel! sa- rò tuo sal- va-tor, po- pol fiam-mingo, io
swear: It is I, I a- lone, Through whom Flan-ders shall

46224

185

186

ALL°. più moderato di prima ♩= 80
D.CARLO
(Don Carlos hands the sword to Rodrigo who bows and presents it to the King.)
O ciel! Tu! Rodrigo!
Oh God! You... Rod-ri-go?
V ALL°. più moderato di prima ♩= 80
ELI.
Ei!
He!
FIL.
Marchese, Duca sie-te. An-diam or al-la fe-sta.
Mar-quis, from now on duke! And now let us pro-ceed!
Sop.
Egli! Posa!
He?... Po-sa!
Ten.
Egli! Posa!
He?... Po-sa!
Bassi
Egli! Posa!
He?... Po-sa!
CHORUS
AI WHISPER
(The King, taking the Queen's hand, resumes the procession. Their entourage follows them to their seats where they are to watch the Auto-da-Fé.)
F
I°. TEMPO
I°. TEMPO

CHORUS OF PEOPLE
Sop.I.
Sop.II.
Ten.I.
Ten.II.
Bassi
ff
cres.
Spun-ta - to è il dì d'e - sul-tan - za, o-nor, o-
May long live the King! His prais - es we sing In grate - ful pros-
Spun-ta - to è il dì d'e - sul - tan - za, o-nor, al Re, o-
May long live the King! As prais - es we sing In grate - ful pros-
As his prais - es we sing In grate - ful pros-

nor al Re! In es so han no i po pol fi
tra tion. We pledge him to day that loy al we
nor al Re! In es so hanno i po pol fi dan
tra tion. We pledge him that loy al we stay, His
nor al Re! In es so han no i po pol fi
tra tion. We pledge him to day that loy al we
nor al Re! In es so hanno i po pol fi dan
tra tion. We pledge him that loy al we stay, His
nor al Re! In es so han no i po pol fi
tra tion. We pledge him to day that loy al we stay, His
dan za, il mon do è prostra to al suo piè!
stay, His fame be found and his name be renowned to the end of Cre-a tion!
za, il mon do è prostra to al suo piè!
fame be found and renowned to the end of Cre-a tion!
dan za, il mon do è prostra to al suo piè!
stay, His fame be found and his name be renowned to the end of Cre-a tion!
za, il mon do è prostra to al suo piè!
fame be found and his name be renowned to the end of Cre-a tion!
dan za, il mon do è prostra to al suo piè!
fame be found and his name be renowned to the end of Cre-a tion!
Z
p
p

6 FRATI

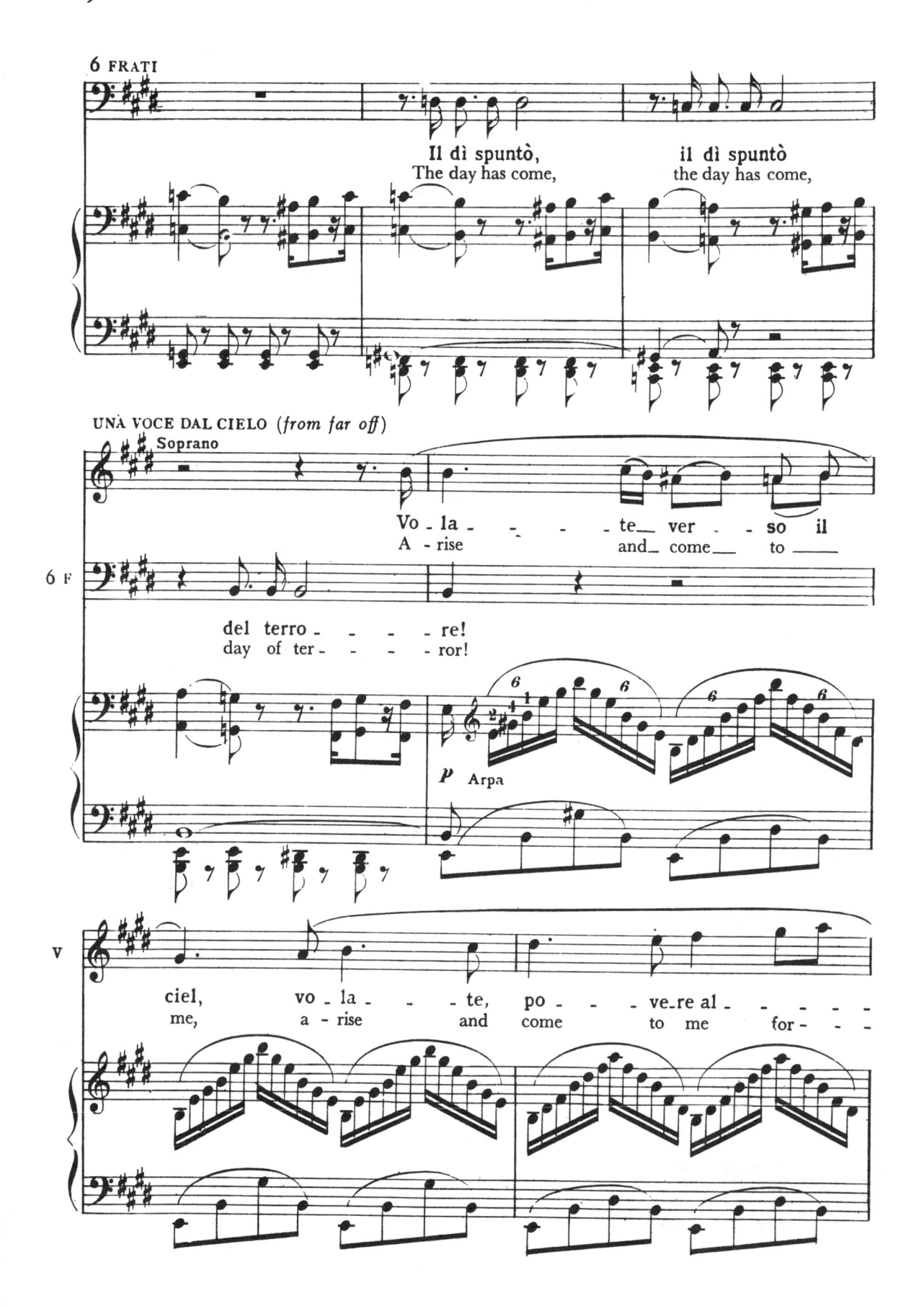

Il dì spuntò, il dì spuntò
The day has come, the day has come,

UNA VOCE DAL CIELO (*from far off*) — Soprano

Vo—la—te— ver—so il ciel, vo—la—te, po—ve—re al—
A—rise and— come— to— me, a—rise and come to me for—

6 F

del terro—— —re!
day of ter— —ror!

p Arpa

191

192

perdendosi
V
FIL.
ff
Glo_ _ria al ciel! gloria al ciel!
Glo- - -ry be! Glo - ry be!
6 D
E tu lo soffri, o ciel!
And Heav- -en can look on!
6 F
ff
Glo_ _ria al ciel! glo_ria al ciel!
Glo- - -ry be! Glo- - ry be!
Sop.
ff
Glo - ria al ciel!
ff Glo - - -ry be!
Ten.
Glo - ria al ciel!
ff Glo - - -ry be!
Bassi
CORO
Glo - ria al ciel!
Glo - - -ry be!
(The stake goes up in flames.)
ff
(Curtain.)

ACT THREE

PART ONE

The King's study in Madrid.

195

(Curtain.)
Philip II, deep in thought, sitting at a table strewn with papers. Two candles are nearly burnt down. Dawn starts breaking, lighting the window.

FILIPPO *(as if in a dream)*

|A|

Ella giammai m'a-mò! no! quel cor chiu-so m'è, a-mor per me non
I nev-er won her heart! No! It nev-er was mine, Her heart was nev-er

46224

ha, perme non ha! Io la ri_ve_do an_
mine, Was nev-er mine! I still can see her

_cor contemplar triste in vol _ to il mio crin bianco il dì che qui di Francia
eyes Look-ing, sad and be_-wil-dered, At my grey hair, when first she came from France to

ven _ ne.
meet me.

No, amor perme non ha! A_mor per me non ha! Ove
No, her heart was nev-er mine, Her heart was nev _ _ er mine! Where

197

mia giornata è giunta a se—ra, dor—mi—rò sol sot—to la vôl—ta
peace, My jour-ney will be end—ed. Night will en—fold The one whose soul as-

ne—ra, dor—mirò sotto la vôl— — ta ne—ra, là nell'a—vello dell'Escuri—
cend— ed On—ward to God, the Lord in Heav-en, Out of the si-lent tomb at Escu—

—al. Se il serto regal a me
—rial. Why can-not the crown Lend my

des—se il po—ter di leg—ge—re nei cor, che Dio può
search-ing eyes the pow'r To read the hu-man heart's In-ner-most

199

re, il consor- te l'o-no-re!
crown, And his wife, and his hon-or.

a tempo cantabile
Dor-mi-rò sol nel manto mio re-gal, quan-do la
Lone-ly and cold, Laid out in shrouds of gold, I shall find

mia giorna-ta è giunta a se-ra, dor-mi-rò sol sot-to la vôl-ta
peace, My jour-ney will be end-ed. Night will en-fold The one whose soul as-

ne-ra, dor-mirò sotto la vôl- -ta ne-ra, là nell'avello dell'Escuri-
cend-ed On-ward to God, the Lord in Heav-en, Out of the si-lent tomb at Escu-

al.
rial.

Ah! se il serto regal
Ah! Why can-not the crown

a me desse il po-ter di leg-ge-re nei cor!
Lend my sens-es the pow'r To read the hu-man heart?!

lungo silenzio

Ella giammai mi a-mò! no! quel cor chiuso m'è, a-mor per me non
I knew it long a-go Now I doubt it no more! Her heart was nev-er

(*He again loses himself in his thoughts.*)

ha, a-mor per me non ha!
mine, Her heart was nev-er mine!

(The Grand Inquisitor, ninety years old and blind, enters. He is supported by two Dominican friars.)
LARGO ♩ = 56
IL CONTE DI LERMA
Il Grand'Inquisi_tor!
The Grand In- -quis-itor!
f
pp
pp legato
FILIPPO
Sì; vi feci chiamar mio.
Yes. I bade youcome here, my
L'INQUISITORE
Son io dinanzi al Re?
Am I be-fore the King?
dim.
F
padre! In dubbio io son.
fa-ther. I am in doubt.
Carlo mi colma il cor
Car-los has plunged my heart
d'u_na tristezza a_
In- to de-spair and
pp
pp
pp

203

INQ. ...ma...ra; sadness. l'Infant'è a me ri...bel...le, ar mossi contro il padre. He e-ven drew his sword A-gainst his roy-al fa-ther.

Qual mezzo per punir scegli tu?
What pun-ish-ment can fit such a crime?

F: Mezzo estrem. Che fugga... o che la scu...re...
On - ly one! While flee-ing... by ex-e-cu-tion...

I: Noto mi sia!
But in what way?

F: Se il figlio a morte invio, m'assolve la tua ma...no?
If I per-mit his death, Can I ob-tain your par-don?

I: Ebben? La pa...ce dell'im...
Well then? The safe-ty of the

Posso il figlio immolar al mondo, io cristian?
How can I, a Christian father, Kill my son?

Per riscattarci Iddio il suo sacrificò.
God, in order to redeem us, Has sacrificed His own.

L'impero di val d'un ribelle.
kingdom Does not allow rebellion.

Ma tu puoi dar vigor a legge sì severa?
But how can you sustain A law so harsh and fearful?

Ovunque avrà vigor, se sul Calvario
What Calvary sustained Does not demand my

205

Nell'ispano suol mai l'eresia dominò, ma v'ha chi vuol minar l'edifizio divin. L'amico egli è del Re, il suo fedel compagno, il dèmon tentator che lo spinge a rovina. Di Carlo il tradimento, che giunse a t'irritar, in paragon del suo futile gioco ap-

Never here in Spain has heresy won ground, Despite the cunning schemes Of the foes of our Faith. But now the King himself Has chosen as companion A most dangerous fiend bent on nothing but treason. Don Carlos' own rebellion, Which comes to bitter end, Seems innocent and childish when compared to your

-par. Ed io,___ l'Inqui_si_tor, io che le_va_i so_
friend. And I___ re-main a-lone, Heav-en's de-vout__ de-

_ven_te sopra or_ de vil' di rei la ma_ no mia pos_
fend-er, More might-y than the throne And all___ its pomp and

_sen_te, pei grandi di quag_giù, scordan_do la mia
splen-dor: Here I stand i-dly by, While loud with trea-son

fè, tranquilli lascio andar___ un gran ri_bel___le... e il
ring The voic-es of the trai-tor And his pa___-tron, the

FIL.
I.º TEMPO
Per traver - sar i dì do-lenti in cui vi - viamo nella mia Cor - te in-
In times like these the King him-self needs someone near him, Oth-er than those at
I
Re.
King!
D
pp I.º TEMPO
F
-van cercat'ho quel che bramo. Un uomo! Un cor le - al... Io lo tro-
court, Who fawn be-cause they fear him, A man, a trust-ed friend, And I have
-vai!
found one.
INQ.
Perchè un uo - mo? Perchè al - lor il nome hai tu di
You need a friend? Why then grand-ly call your-self a
p
col canto
Non più, fra -
E-nough, Priest!
Re, Si - re, s'al-cun v'ha pa - ri a te?
king, Sire, if you feel a need for e-quals?

ALL° AGITATO MOSSO ♩=132

Le i_dee dei no_va_tor in te son pe_ne_trate!
Al-read-y I per-ceive The can-ker of sub-ver-sion!

In_frange_re tu vuoi con la tua de_bol man
The spir-it of dis-sent Now rules the roy-al home,

il san_to giogo e_steso sovra l'orbe ro_man!
To break the gen-tle yoke That ties the world to Rome!

Ri_tor_na al tuo do_ver; la Chiesa all'uom che
Your du-ty now is clear. The Church can ease the

spe-ra, a chi si pen-te, puote offrir la venia inte-ra:
sen-tence Of sin-ners who con-fess And pine in true re-pen-tance.

FIL.

ppp

No, giammai!
No, not that!

a te chie-do il Si-gnor di Po-sa.
I de-mand that you hand me Po-sa!

♩ = 152
UN POCO PIÙ ANIMATO

ff

ff ♩ = 152
UN POCO PIÙ ANIMATO

Re, se non fos-s'io con te nel regio o-stel oggi
King, had you not called me here To hear your se - - cret con-

stesso, lo giu-ro a Dio, doman sa-re-sti presso il
fes-sion, I swear to God, you would ap-pear Be-fore the

211

I
-sen - - - - - - te! L'opra di tan-ti dì tu vuoi strugger, de-
joy it. What in de-vo-tion I wrought, Must your fol-ly de-
I
-men - - - - - - - te!
stroy it?!
f
ff
I
Per-chè mi trovo io qui?
But why am I still here?
Che vuol il Re da
What is the King's com-
pp
FIL.
I.º TEMPO
Mio pa-dre, che tra
(He is about to leave.)
My Fa-ther, let be-
I
me?
mand?
I.º TEMPO
pp
H
pp
pp

noi la pace alberghi an_cor. Obbliar tu
tween us A-gree-ment be re-stored! You must for-
(He proceeds on his way out.)

La pa_ce?
A - gree-ment?

dêi quel ch'è pas_sa_to. Dunque il
get all that was spo-ken. *(in the doorway)* Will the

For - - se!
Must I?

tro_no piegar do_vrà sempre all'al_ta _ re!
crown ca-pit-u-late a-gain Before the al - tar?!

214

𝅗𝅥 = 108
ALL⁰. AGITATO

ELISABETTA *(The Queen enters, very excited, and throws herself at the King's feet.)*

|A| Giusti _ zia, giusti _ zia, Si _ re! Giu _
Oh help me, oh help me, Sire! For

_ stizia, giu_stizia! Ho fè nel_la leal_tà del
jus-tice I plead... The King will not de-ny my

46224

[B] Re. Son nel la Cor te tu a cru del men te trat ta ta e da ne mi ci o scu ri, in co gni ti ol trag gia ta. [C] Lo scrigno ov'io chiu de a, Si re, tutt'un te sor, i gio iel li altri og

right. A-round me here at court I find dis like and def a ma tion, And now an act of in fa my Has roused my in dig na tion: The cas ket, in which I keep, Sire, the pearls I own, Dif-f'rent ob jects, trea sured

D
EL.
-get-ti a me più ca- -ri an-cor, l'hanno ra-pi - to a
keep-sakes Of worth to my-self a - lone, 'T has dis-ap-peared, my
me! l'hanno ra-pi - to a me! Giu-sti - zia, giu-
Lord. I have been robbed, my Lord! Oh, help me to
-sti - zia! la re-cla-mo da Vostra Ma-e-stà.
find it! I de-mand it of your Maj-es-ty, the King!
FILIPPO (The King rises slowly, takes a casket from the table, offers it to the Queen.)
Quello che voi cer-
What you have lost, my
E
Ciel!
Ah!
F
-ca-te, ec-co-lo! A voi d'aprir-lo
La-dy, Here it is. I beg you to un-

(The Queen makes a sign of refusal.)
(He breaks open the casket.)
F
piaccia.
lock it.
F
Ebben, io l'a_pri _ rò!
I o-pen it my-self!
f
ff
ELI.
(aside)
(Ah! mi sento morir!)
(Ah! May God be with me!)
F
Il ri_trat_to di Carlo!
'Tis the por-trait of Car-los!
parlato
G
MODERATO ♩=104
F
Non trova _ te pa _ rola?
Would you care to ex - plain it?
Il ri_trat _to di Carlo!
'Tis the por - trait of Car-los!
MODERATO ♩=104
p
ELI.
Sì!
Yes.
Sì!
Yes.
F
Fra i vo_stri gio _ iel'?
A - midst all your pearls?

EL.
F
MOD.to ♩=80
Io l'o_so! sì! Ben lo sa_
I dare it, yes! Have you for-
Che! confes_sar l'o_sa_te a me?
What! And you dare con-firm your guilt?
H
_pete, un dì pro_mes_sa al figlio vo_stro fu la mia man! or v'appar_
got-ten That once to Car-los In sol-emn prom-ise Was pledged my life? Now, by the
Cantabile
PIÙ ANIMATO
_ten_go a Di_o som_mes_sa,_ ma im_maco_la_ta qual giglio
ho_ly will of the Al-might_y,_ I am your vir-tuous and loy-al
son!_ Ed o_ra si so_spetta l'onor d'Eli_sa_betta! si du_bi_ta di
wife._ But now my foes suspect me, and he who should protect me adds poi son to their
PIÙ MOSSO ♩=112
I
me... e chi m'ol_trag_gia è il Re!
sting, My no-ble hus-band, the King!

219

UN POCO MENO MOSSO

FIL. Ardita troppo voi favellate! me debole crede te e sfidarmi sembrate; la debolezza in me può diventar furor. Tremate allor per voi, per me!

Your every gesture bespeaks defiance! No doubt you now are certain Of my humble compliance. But my restraint may turn To wildly flaming rage. Then Heaven help both you and me!

ELI. Il mio fallir qual è? crime? Spergiura! se tanta infamia colmò la mi

But what has been my 'Tis perjury! If you reviled And betrayed what is

46224

F
_su _ ra,
sa - cred;
M
se fui da
If you de -
mf
ff
voi, ___ se fui tradi - - - to,
filed ___ our ho-ly u - - - nion,
N
io lo giu _ ro, lo giuro innanzi al ciel, il san_gue ver - - se_
Then I swear it, I swear by God on high, To drown my shame in
ELI.
Pietà mi fa_te
You raise my pit-y!
a piacere
_rò! Ah! la pie_tà ___ d'a_dul_te_ra con_
blood! Ah! Spare your pit-y, The pit-y of a
dim. col canto

ALLEGRO ♩ = 132
(fainting)
EL.
Ah!
Ah!
(opening the door to the rear)
F
O
- sor - te!
har - lot!
Soc - corso alla Re -
Some-one to help the
ff ALLEGRO ♩ = 132
F
- gi - - na!
Queen!
f
EBOLI (terrified at seeing the Queen lying unconscious)
P
ff
(Ciel! che mai
(Ah! God for -
f dim.
EB.
fe - ci! Ahi - mè!)
give me! My Queen!)
p

RODRIGO (*to the King*)

Si — re! sogget — ta è a voi la me — tà del la ter — ra: sa — re — ste dun — que in tan to va — — — sto im per il sol — cui non v'è da — to il co — man — dar?

Sire, you wield the pow'r O — — ver mil — lions of hu — — mans: Can it be true, That in this vast do — main the one — Whom you have failed to com-mand Is you?

FIL.
LARGO ♩=58
(aside)
R
LARGO ♩=58
p
(Ah! sii ma-le-detto, so-spet-to fa-ta-le, o-pera d'un de-mòn, d'un demòn in-fer-nal!
(In-fer-nal sus-pi-cion, E-ter-nal per-di-tion; Cursed be this e-vil spell Of a de-mon in Hell!
F
EBOLI
(La perdei! la perdei! Oh rimor-so fa-ta-le! Commettea, commettea un delitto infer-nal! la perdei! la per-
(It is I, it is I, Who have doomed her for-ev-er! What I did, What I did is too monstrous a crime! Let me die! Let me
parlante a mezzavoce
No! no! non macchiò la fè giu-rata... la sua fierezza il dice a me!)
No, no! She could not, could not be-tray me. Her no-ble bear-ing can-not lie.)
EB.

EB.
-dei!)
die!)
ROD. (aside)
S
(Omai d'oprar suonata è l'o-ra, folgor or-renda in ciel bril-
(The time is here! All doubt has end-ed. A flash of light-ning Has rent the
R
-lò, o-mai d'oprar suonata è l'o-ra, folgor or-ren-da in ciel bril-
sky, And with-out fear, As Fate in-tend-ed, For God and Right I have to
EBOLI
(La per-de-i ri-mor-so fa-
(Let me die in shame and dis-
R
-lo! Che per la Spa-gna un uomo muora... lieto avve-nir le la-sce-
die! And with-out fear, As Fate in-tend-ed, For God and Right I have to
FIL.
(A me in-fe-
(Her heart is

225

ELI.
(coming to)
Che avven-ne? O
Where am I? Oh
EB.
cor! oh dolor! oh! do-lor!
heart. Let me die! Oh, to die!
R
-prar suonata è l'o - - - ra!)
here! All doubt has end - - - ed.)
F
-de - le infe-dele non fu!)
grad - - ed what is no-ble and true.)
EL.
ciel! in pian-to e duo - - - lo
Heav-en! In pain and sor - - - row,
EL.
o - gnun, o ma - dre, m'ab - bando-nò. Io
EBOLI Far from the land I knew long a-go, A-
Oh do - lor!)
Oh, my heart!)

EL.
son stra_nie_ra in que - - sto suol!
lone, for-sak-en, in dark - - est night!
dolcissimo
EL.
più sul - la ter - - ra spe - me non
EBOLI All now has end - - -ed But tor-ment, and
(Ri - mor - - - so, rimor - so fa -
Ah, vain re- - morse is haunt - ing my
EL.
ho!
woe!
EB.
-tal! la tradia! io tradia quel no - bi - le
heart! It is I who be-trayed and have bro - ken her
ROD.
(Omai d'oprar suonata è l'ora, folgor orrenda in ciel bril -
(The time is here! All doubt has end-ed. A flash of lightning Has rent the
FIL.
(No non macchiò la fè giu - ra - ta, a me in-fe -
(No, now I know she nev - er be - trayed me, Nev - er de -
U
ppp leggero

dolcissimo
EL.
Ah! so_la, stra_
Ah, lone-ly, for-
dolciss.
EB.
core! io ne morrò, dal dolor mor_rò! i - o tradi - a quel no_bi - le
heart! Ah, Let me die of de-spair and woe! I be-trayed and doomed her for
R
- lò, in ciel, in ciel bril_lò!
sky, lit up the sky, the sky!
F
- de - le infe_dele non fu!
grad - ed what is no-ble and true.
V
EL.
- nie - ra in que - sto suo - lo, ah! più sul - la
sak - en, In pain and sor - row, Ah, all now has
EB.
co - re, oh! do_lor! oh! do - lor! io la tra_di - va! ah! ne mor_
ev - er! Oh, what pain Oh, what woe! I have be-trayed her. Ah, let me
R
e che per la Spagna un uo - mo mora
And with - out fear, As my Fate in - tend-ed,
F
No! non mac_chiò
No, now I know

EL.
ter - ra spe - me non ho, ognun, ahimè! o ma - dre
end - ed in tor - ment and woe! A-lone, I suf-fer in pain and
EB.
- rò! io la tradia! Ah! ne morrò, la per - dei, la
die! Yes, I must die Ah, Let me die! I shall die for
R
lie-to av-ve - nir le la - sce - rò! che
For God and Right I shall have to die! I
F
la fè giu - ra - ta! a me in - fe -
she did not shame me, did not de -
EL.
mi - a, ognun quaggiù m'abban - do - nò, più spe - me o -
an-guish. Oh, take me back, o land of mine! Here I shall
EB.
tra - dia! oh! ri - mor - so fa - ta - le! io tra - dia quel no - bi - le
my lie. My re - morse is in vain For I be-trayed and doomed her for-
R
per la Spa - gna un uo - mo mora, io lie - ti dì le la - sce
die for Spain and for Car - los, And in the sky the sign of free-dom shall
F
- del co - ste - i non fu!
grade what's no - ble and true.
cresc.

dim.
dolciss.
dim.
EL.
-mai ah! che in ciel, in ciel non
die! Ah! Heav - en, end my tor-ment and
EB.
co-re! oh! do-lor! oh ri-mor - so! io ne mor-
ev - er! Ah, to die! Ah, what tor - ment Ah, let me
R
-rò, io lie - ti dì, io lie - ti dì le la - sce-
fly! Yes, in the sky up high the sign of free - dom
F
a me non fu, non fu, in - fe - del, ah! no! a me non
She did not shame and did not de - grade what's pure, no-ble and
pp
allarg.
a tempo
EL.
ho! spe - me ho
woe! Heav'n a
EB.
-rò! oh! ri-morso fa-tal! oh! ri-morso fa-tal!
die! My re-morse is in vain, My re-morse is in vain,
R
-rò! Ch'un uo - mo
fly! One man shall
F
fu! Ah sia ma - le - detto il sospet - to, il de -
true. In - fer - nal sus - pi-cion, E - ter - nal per -
Z
a tempo
p
mf
p
f

EL. sol — speme ho sol — ho — sol nel ciel!
lone, — Heaven a-lone, — Heaven can end my woe!

EB. se più perdon non avrò in terra, o in ciel!)
never before have I known grief that now I know!)

R. mora, lieti di a lei legar saprò!)
die — For God and Right, So freedom shall never die!)

F. mone, il ri - o de - mon!)
di-tion; You de-mon from Hell!)

(*After a moment of hesitation, the King leaves. With an obvious gesture of decision, Rodrigo follows him. Eboli remains alone with the Queen.*)

EBOLI (*throwing herself at the Queen's feet*)

Pie -
My

232

A
EB.
cor. An - gel del ciel, Re - gi - - na augusta e
torn. An - - gel of light, my Queen, My roy - al
p
EB.
pi - a, sap - pia - - - te a qual de - món l'in -
La - dy: Your eyes are now be - hold - ing A
f
p
B
EB.
- fer - no vi - dà in preda! Quello scrigno son io che l'invo -
Fu - ry sent by Sa - tan. Your cas - ket! 'Twas I who stole it,
Recit.
f
p col canto
ELI.
Presto
Voi!
You?
Voi!
You?
EB.
- lai. Sì, son io, son io che v'accu - sa - i!
I! Yes, for I had turned in - to a spy!
Recit.
Presto
f
p col canto
Presto
f

C
EBOLI
Sì L'amor, il fu-ror l'odio che avea per voi la ge-lo-sia cru-del che strazia-vami il cor contro voi m'ecci-tàr!
Yes. What love could not pos sess, My ha-tred would de-stroy! Rav-ing in jeal ous de-spair I no long-er could bear The dis-tress of my heart!
p cresc. f p ff
EB.
Io Carlo a-mava! E Car-lo m'ha sprezzata! No! no! pie-tà di me! un' al-tra col-pa!
I loved Don Car-los, And Car-los did re-ject me! No, no! My Queen, for-give me! I have not told you
ELI.
Voi l'a-maste! Sor-gete! Ancor!
You have loved him? A-rise! What more?!
pp p f ff

EBOLI MODERATO ♩= 92
D MODERATO ♩= 92
pp cupo
Pietà! pie_
Ah, mer-cy!
pp
_tà! Il Re... non impre_cate a
Mer-cy! The King... Your eyes im-pale my
ff con forza
me! sì! se_dotta! per_duta! l'er_
heart! I, disgraced and for-sak-en... The
ppp con voce soffocata
_ror che v'impu_tai... io... io stessa... a_vea... com_
crime I blamed on you... I, my La-dy, have wrought my-
pp dim.

UN POCO PIU MOSSO ♩ = 112
EB.
- messo!
self!
E
UN POCO PIÙ MOSSO ♩ = 112
ff
dim.
pp
ELI.
(Eboli hands it to her.)
Rende-temi la cro-ce!
The cru-ci-fix I gave you!
morendo
p
ppp
EL.
La Corte vi con-vien lasciar col dì no-vel-lo!
You will de-part from court Be-fore the day is o-ver!
p
ppp
EL.
(The Queen leaves. Eboli rises.)
Fra l'esi-lio ed il vel sceglier po-trete!
Between ex-ile and veil You have the choice!
p
pp

ALLEGRO
EBOLI (in despair)
Ah! più non vedrò ah più mai non vedrò la Re-
Ah! The Queen has left me, And now I have lost her for-
F
ff ALLEGRO
p
ALL°. GIUSTO ♩= 84
EB.
-gi - na!
- ev - er!
ALL°. GIUSTO ♩= 84
f ff
ff
EB.
O don fa-ta-le, o don cru-del che in suo fu-
O, dole of dark-ness, O, boon of Hell, That in his
p
EB.
-ror mi fe-ce il cie - - lo! Tu che ci fa-i sì va-ne, al-
fu-ry Has fash-ioned a de - - mon! You wrought my beau-ty To cast your
p

con forza
cres.
EB.
-tere, ti ma-le-di-co, ti male-di - - co,o mia-bel-
spell! Vain-ly I curse you, Vain-ly I curse your gift from
f
PIÙ MOSSO ♩=126
-tà. Versar,ver-sar sol pos-so il pian-to, speme non
G
Hell! My bit-ter tears, my des-o-la-tion, My tor-tured
p
ho, sof-frir do-vrò! Il mio de-lit-to è orri-bil
mind, my heart dis-traught! All my re-pen-tance, my des-per-
tan-to che can-cel-lar mai nol po-trò! Ti male-
a-tion Can-not-un-do what I have wrought! Fa-vor from
H

EB.
-di - co, ti male-di - co, o mia bel-tà, ah! ti ma-le - dico, o mia bel-
Sa - tan, vain-ly I curse you! Beau-ty of mine, ah! Vain-ly I curse you, beau-ty from
f
f
EB.
-tà.
Hell!
f
p
MOLTO MENO ♩ = 84
EB.
cantabile
I
O — mia Re-gi - na, io t'im - mo - la - i al — fol - le er-
Lone - ly and re - gal, oh see — my — cry - ing, You — whom my
MOLTO MENO ♩ = 84
p
f
EB.
pp
-ror — di — que-sto cor. So-lo in un chio - stro al mondo or-
mad - ness sought — to — de-stroy Pride, once so haugh - ty, sin - ful and
p

EB.
f
J
pp
-ma - i do - vrò-ce-lar il - mio do - lor! Ohi-mè! Ohi-
ly - ing, Now-turned to shame, to - gloom my - joy! Fare-well, fare-
f
pp
EB.
-mè! O mia Re-gi-na, so - lo in un chio - stro
well, my Queen, for - ev - er! Si - lent, the clois - ter
EB.
string.
cres.
al - mondo o-ma - i do - vrò - ce - lar il - mi-o do - lo - re!
Wit-ness my tor-ment, Hear - my - re - pen-tance, End - less, un-dy - ing,
string.
cres.
largamente
EB.
Ah! solo in un chiostro al mon-do o-mai dovrò ce-lar il mi-o do-
ah! On-ly the clois-ter Shall know my de-spair, And God a-lone shall hear me
col canto

ALL.º PIÙ MOSSO ♩ = 152
EB.
-lor!
cry!
L
ALL.º PIÙ MOSSO ♩ = 152
mf
f
Oh ciel! E Carlo? a morte do-
Oh God! And Car-los? He per-ish... To-
p
-mani... gran Dio! a morte andar ve-drò!
mor-row, and I my-self Shall be to blame?
cres.
lunga
Ah! un dì mi resta, la spe-me m'ar-ri-de,
Ah, I still can save him! One ray of hope is shin-ing!
f
col canto
ff

con slancio
EB.
si - - - a be-ne-det - - - - to il ciel, benedet-to il
M
Heav- - - - en, oh help me now! Oh help me
ciel! Lo-sal-ve-rò! Un dì mi resta, un dì mi-
now! He must be free! I still can save him! I still can
resta, ah si - - - a benedet - to il ciel!
save him! O Heav- - en, help me now! Oh God!
cres.
(exits quickly)
Lo sal-ve-rò!..
He shall be free!

ACT THREE

PART TWO

The prison of Don Carlos.

A dark dungeon, hastily furnished with a few appropriate objects. Through the iron bars which separate the prison from the courtyard beyond we see guards pacing up and down. A small stairway leads from the courtyard up to the higher parts of the building.

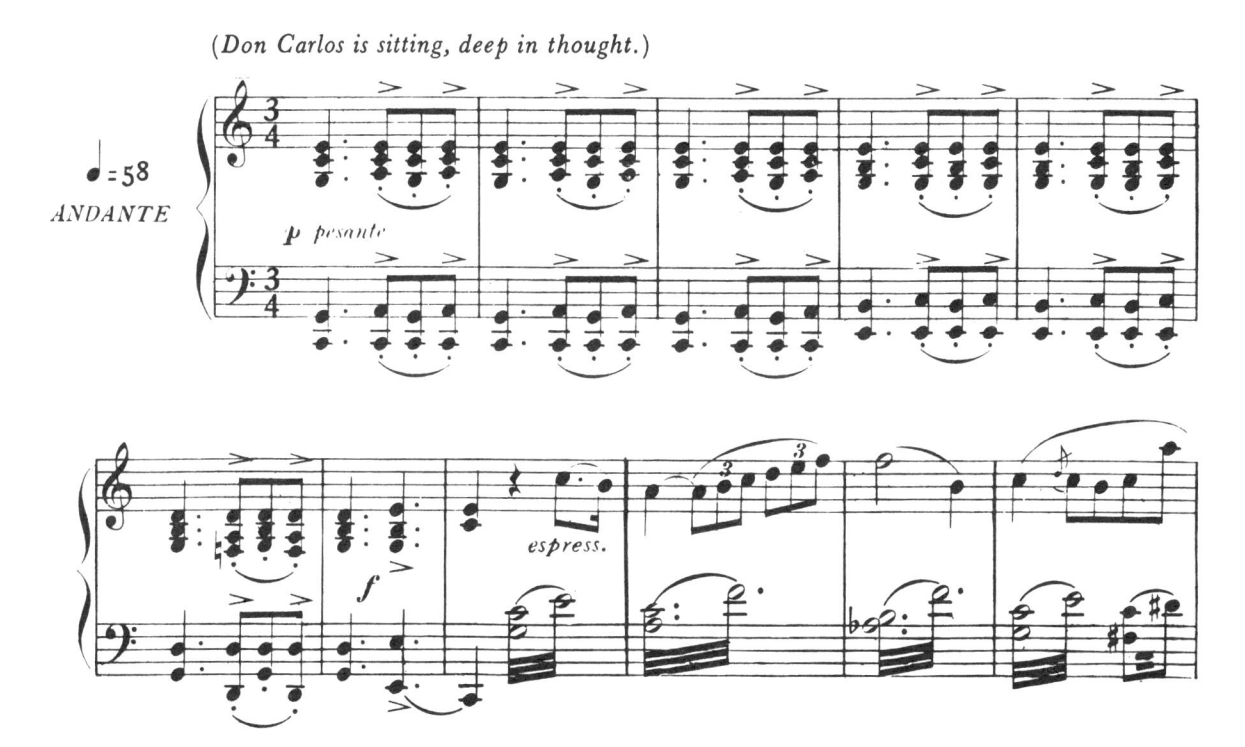

(Don Carlos is sitting, deep in thought.)

(Rodrigo enters, whispering to some officials who withdraw immediately. He sadly looks at Carlos who, aware of a visitor, moves slightly.)

244

245

ROD. Ah! noto appien ti sia l'affetto mio! Uscir tu déi da quest'orrendo avel. Felice ancor io son se abbracciar ti poss'io! Io ti salvai! Convien qui dirci, convien qui dirci addio. O mio Carlo!

Carlos, you fill my heart With grief and sorrow. But you will leave This place of gloom and death. And yet, my heart is glad For the chance to behold you. I saved your life! 'Tis for the last time, For we shall part forever. O, my Carlos!

D. CARLO Che di'? My life? *(deeply moved)*

(Don Carlos is stunned and looks at Rodrigo without making a move.)

ANDte SOSTENUTO ♩ = 58
cantabile
R
Per me giun - - to è il dì su - - pre - mo, no, mai
Yes, my life will soon be end - ed, And we
A ANDte SOSTENUTO ♩ = 58
pp
più ci ri - - - ve - drem; ci con - - giun - - ga Id - dio nel
nev - - - er meet a - gain Till to God we - have as -
dolce
pp
ciel, Ei che pre - - mia i suoi fe - - del'.
cend - ed, Re - - u - nit - - - ed in His reign.
espress.
Sul tuo ci - - glio il pian - - to io
On your brow I see your

mi - ro; la - gri - mar, la - grimar co sì per-
sor - row. Bit - ter tears, bit - ter tears your eyes be-

-chè? No, fa cor, no, fa cor, l'estre - mo
dew. Oh, take heart, yes, take heart! Al-might-y

spi - ro, l'e - stre mo spi - ro lieto e a
Heav - en will smile up - on him, Who gave his

chi, a chi morrà, morrà per te. No, fa cor, no, fa
life Who gave his life to die for you. So take heart, so take

248

249

Ri_volta ho già su me la fol_go_re tre_menda! Tu più non
The tide has turned, and I Am now the lead-ing cul-prit. You now are

sei oggi il ri_val del Re; il fiero a_gi_ta_tor del_le
free Of all dis-trust and doubt: He who has wrought re-bel-lion In

D. CARLO

Chi po_trà pre_star fè?
Who be-lieves such a lie?

Fiandre son io! Le pro_ve son tre_
Flan-ders 'tis I! The proof is o-ver-

a tempo

_men_de! I fogli tuoi tro_vati in mio po_ter
whelm-ing: All your pa-pers were found in my pos-ses-sion,

46224

250

R
tu la dovra - i com - pi - re Un nuo - - - vo se - col
You are their sole de - fend - er. In bright and ra - diant
d'ôr ri - na - scer tu fa - rai;
splen - - dor Our dream will yet come true!
dim.
re - gna - re tu do - ve - vi, ed io morir per
Your life be - longs to free - dom, While I must die for
ALL°. MOSSO ♩=152
D. CARLO (The man carrying the firearm has taken aim at Rodrigo and fires.)
(terrified)
Ciel! la morte! per chi
God! A bul - let . . . but for
te.
you.
♩=152
ALL°. MOSSO
ff

mai? / whom?

(mortally wounded)

Per me! / For me...

La vendetta del Re / the revenge of the King...

(sinking into Carlos' arms)

tardare non potea! / ...he did not lose a moment!

Gran Dio! / Oh God!

ASSAI MOD.ᵗᵒ ♩=60

cantabile espress.

ROD.

O Carlo, a— / One word yet, my

-scolta, la ma- -dre t'aspet-ta a San Giusto do-
Car-los... Your moth- -er a-waits you At the clois-ter to-

-man; tutto el-la sa... Ah! la terra mi manca...
day. She has been told... Ah my sens-es are wan-ing...

Carlo mio, a me porgi la man!
O, my friend, once more Give me your hand!

Io mor- -rò, ma lie- -to in
I shall die hap- -py, con-

co - - re, chè po -
tent - - ed, For I

- tei co - sì ser
give my life for

- bar al - la
Spain. Car - los'

Spa - - gna un sal - va -
death I have pre -

-to — — — re! Ah! di —
vent — — ed, And his —

me... non — ti scor — dar!..
stars shine — once a — gain!

PIÙ MOSSO *(ma un poco meno di prima)*
♩=76

parlato

Di me... non ti scordar!
My friend... re-mem-ber me!

Regna — re tu do — ve vi, ed io mo — rir per
Your life be-longs to free - dom, And I must die for

col canto

te. Ah! Io morrò, ma lieto in
you, ah! I shall die happy, con-

co— — —re, chè po—
tent— — —ed, For I

—tei cosi ser
give my life for

—bar alla Spagna un salva—
Spain. Car—los' death I have pre—

R
-to-re! Ah! di me non ti..scor-
vent-ed, And his stars shine once a-
f
ALLEGRO ♩=120
R
-dar! Ah! la ter-ra mi man-ca la ma-no a
gain! Ah! I see you no long-er... Give me your
ALLEGRO ♩=120
f
R
me a me. Ah! salva la Fiandra..Carlo, addi-o, ah! ah!
hand, your hand. Ah, Re-mem-ber Flan-ders, Car-los! Farewell, ah! fare-
f
pp
PIÙ MOSSO
(Rodrigo dies. Carlos throws himself across his lifeless body. King Philip enters with the Count of Lerma, Eboli, and other people of his entourage.)
R
well!
PIÙ MOSSO
ff

258

D.C
-cò!
FIL. death!
Pre - sa - gio mio fe - - - ral!
My son, I lose him, too!
G
D.CAR.
Tu più fi - glio non hai! I re - gni mie - i stan pres - so a
Do not call me your son! No tie is left be-tween you and
(looking at Rodrigo)
D.C
lui!
FIL. me!
Chi rende a me quel - l'uom, chi rende a me quel -
Where can I find a - new A man so great and
VELOCISSIMO ♩. = 138
(The storm-bells are heard.)
F
H
- l'uom?
true?
VELOCISSIMO ♩. = 138

GRANDI DI SPAGNA
Ten.
CHORUS
Ciel! suona a stormo!
Hear! Such com - mo-tion!
Bassi
Ciel! suona a stormo!
Hear! Such com - mo-tion!
Sop.
CHORUS OF PEOPLE
Dovrà!
At last!
Ten.
(off-stage)
Pe-rir dovrà chi d'ar - re-
Be free at last! Let no one
Bassi
Pe - rir do - vrà o -
Be free at last! No
fe - riam!
To arms!
-star - ci at - ten-ti! fe-riam! fe-riam! fe-riam, non
dare to op - pose us! To arms! To arms! And mor-tal
-gnun che ci ar - re-sti! fe - riam! fe riam sen-za
one shall op - pose us! To arms! To arms! Mor-tal

261

262

263

FIL. Ob--be--di--te! Io lo
I com-mand you. Do as I

(A furious crowd is rushing onstage.)

vo'!
say!

CHORUS OF PEOPLE

Sop.

Ten.
Fe_riam! fe_riam!
To arms! To arms!

Bassi
Fe_riam! fe_
To arms! To

46224

fe-riam!
To arms!
fe-riam, più niun ci ar-resta! fe-riam! feriam!
To arms! No one will op-pose us! To arms! To arms!
-riam! più niun ci ar-resta! fe-riam! fe-
arms! No one will op-pose us! To arms! To
fe-riam!
To arms!
fe-riam, nè te-ma, nè pie-tà! Tre-mar do-
te-ma, o pie-tà!
To arms! May ter-ror strike their heart, Yes, mor-tal
ter-ror strike their heart,
-riam! sen-za te-ma, o pie-tà! Tre-mar do-
arms! Ter-ror shall strike their heart! Yes, mor-tal
M

Tre - - - - -
Ter - - - - -
-vrà e cur- -var la testa da - - - - - -
ter - ror shall strike their heart, Fear
-vrà e cur- -var la testa sì da- -van- ti al
ter - ror shall strike their heart, Fear of the peo-ple's re -
EBOLI (wearing a mask)
(to Don Carlos)
Va! fuggi!
Flee, Car-los!
FIL.
Che vo-
What do you
-mar da-van- ti al po - pol ul - tor!
ror be-fore the peo - ple's re - venge!
-van- - ti al po - pol ul - tor!
of the peo - ple's re - venge!
po - - pol, - al po - pol ul - tor!
venge, of the peo - ple's re - venge!
N

(pointing to Don Carlos)
F
_le_te? Egli qui sta!
want? Here is my son.
L'In_ _fante!
Don Car-los!
L'In_ _fante!
Don Car-los!
L'In_ _fante!
Don Car-los!
INQUISITORE
(appearing suddenly)
ALL° AGITATO ♩=126
Sa_cri_le_gio in_fa_me!
In-fa-my in-fer-nal!
(The people recede before the Grand Inquisitor.)
ff
Il gran In- - -qui_si_tor!
The Grand In- -quis-i-tor!
ff
Il gran In- -qui_si_tor!
The Grand In- -quis-i-tor!
ff
Il gran In- -qui_si_tor!
The Grand In- -quis-i-tor!
O
ALL° AGITATO ♩=126
p
ff

IN.
Vi pro_stra_ _ _ te innan_zi al Re,
On your knees be-fore the King!
pp
f
6
IN.
che Dio pro_teg_ - - - - - - - - - - ge!
The Lord pro-tects him.
P
ff
5
IN.
Vi pro_stra_te! vi prostra_ _te!
On your knees! On your knees!
pp
cres.
p
6
FIL.
A ter- - - - ra!
Sur- ren- - - - der!
IN.
vi pro_stra_ _te! A ter- - - - - ra!
On your knees! Sur- - ren- - - - der!
Q
ff
ppp
f
6

(The people fall to their knees.)
CHORUS OF PEOPLE
pp
Si - gnor, di noi pie - tà!
O Lord! Mer - cy, o Sire!
Si - gnor, di noi pie - tà!
O Lord! Mer - cy, o Sire!
Si - gnor, di noi pie - tà!
O Lord! Mer - cy, o Sire!
PIÙ MOSSO ♩= 144
FIL.
Gran Dio, sia gloria a te!
O God, great is Thy name.
di noi pie - tà! Si
Mer - cy, o Sire! O
R
p

LER.
ff
Ev_viva il Re! Ev_viva il Re!
Long live the King! Long live the King!
FIL.
ff
Gran Dio, glo - - - ria a te!
O God, great Thy name.
INQ.
ff
Gran Dio, glo - - - ria a te!
O God, great Thy name.
CORO
GRANDI DI SPAGNA
(with drawn swords)
ff
Ev_viva il Re!
Long live the King!
ff
Ev_viva il Re!
Long live the King!
ff
- - - - gnor, pie - - - - tà!
Lord! O Lord!
ff
- - - - gnor, pie - - - - tà!
Lord! O Lord!
ff
- - - - gnor, pie - - - - tà!
Lord! O Lord!
cres.
ff

(The Grand Inquisitor descends towards Philip, who goes towards him among the kneeling crowd.)

ACT FOUR

The Cloister of the Monastery of St. Just (same as Act I). It is night, brightened by moonlight.

(Elizabeth enters slowly, absorbed in her thoughts. She approaches the tomb of Charles V and kneels in front of it.)

(s'alza la tela)

272

ALLEGRO AGITATO

ELISABETTA

Tu che le va_ni_tà co_no_sce_sti del mondo e go_di nell'a_vel il ri_po_so_ pro_fondo,
You, who spurned all the might which the world has to of-fer, Who found e-ter-nal peace in this tomb, cold and si-lent!

46224

espressivo
molto dolce
D
s'an - cor si pian - ge in cie - lo, pian - gi sul mio do -
Blind - ed by tears, oh Fa - ther, I raise my eyes to
pp
- lo - re, e por - ta il pian - to mi - o al
Heav - en. Grant me Thy aid And ease my
marcato
cres.
tro - no del Si - gnor, il pian - to
sor - row, gra - cious Lord! Grant me Thy
f
grandioso
mi - o por - ta al tro - no del Si -
aid Ah, ease my sor - row, gra - cious
- gnor.
Lord!
E
pp

ALLEGRO ♩ = 144
Recit.vo
Car - lo qui ver - rà!
Car - los will come soon.
a tempo
ppp
pp
Sì!
Yes,
Che
in
par - ta e scordi oma - i...
Flan-ders he will for - get me.
A Posa di vegliar sui giorni suoi giu -
To Po-sa I had sworn To think of Car-los'
p
a tempo
ALL.o MOD.to ♩ = 100
- ra - i. Ei se - gua il suo de - stin, la glo - ria il trac - ce - rà. Per
fu - ture. He must pur - sue his way, And his stars are shin - ing bright. For
morendo
lungo silenzio
me, la mia gior - na - ta a se - ra è giun - ta già!
me, the days are fad - ing And slow - ly turn to night.
espress.

ALL°. MOD!° PIÙ DI PRIMA ♩=96
E
Fran_cia, no_bi_le
France! O no - ble
ALL°. MOD!° PIÙ DI PRIMA ♩=96
F
p
suol, sì caro a'miei ver_d'an_ni!
soil, That saw my youth-ful yearn - ing . . .
Fon_tai_ne_
My Fon-taine-
_bleau! vêr voi schiu - de il pensier i van_ni. E_
bleau, where my thoughts Are now re - turn - ing. E -
_ter - no giu_ro d'a_mor là Dio da me ascoltò, e quest'e_ter_ni_tà un giorno sol du_
ter - nal love I swore To one who went a-way: E-ter-ni - ty, a - las, did on-ly last a
Lento
f
pp

LARGO ♩=72
E
pp
-rò.
day!
G
Tra voi, va-ghi giardin
Gen-tle gar-dens of Spain,
pp
p
di que - sta ter-ra i-bé-ra, se Carlo ancor do-vrà fer-mar i pas - si a
Whose flow-ers I be-friend-ed, If Car-los once a-gain Should dream of what has
ppp
cres.
se - ra, che le zol - - le, i ruscel -
end - ed, Ev-ery whis - - per, ev-ery sound
pp
f
poco rit.
-li, i fonti, i bo-schi, i fior, con le lor ar-mo-ni - e can-tino il nostro a-
In your ten-der leaves shall re-call That there once was a Queen, Whose love did nev - er
H
cres.
f
col canto

ALL.º AGITATO ♩ = 126
E
-mor. Ad - di - o, ad -
pall! 'Tis o - ver, 'Tis
p
ALL.º AGITATO ♩ = 126
p
-di - o, bei sogni d'ôr, il - lu - sion per -
o - ver, all now is gone, All my hope has
-du - ta! Il no - - - - do si spez -
van - ished. The sky is filled with
I
mf
-zò, la lu - ce, la lu - ce è fat - ta
clouds, And the wings of the night Have de - scend - ed up -

278

I. TEMPO

Tu che le vanità co‑no‑
You, who spurned all the might That the

‑sce‑sti del mon‑‑‑do e
world has to of‑‑‑fer, You

go‑di nel l'a‑vel il ri‑
found e‑ter‑nal peace In this

‑po‑‑‑so pro‑fon‑‑‑do,
tomb, cold and si‑‑‑lent:

dim. *pp morendo*

s'an_cor si pian__ge in cie___lo,
Blind—ed by tears, o Fa—3—ther,

pian_gi sul mio do__lo__re,
I raise my eyes to Heav__3__en!

e por___ta il pian_to mi o al
Grant me Thy aid, Help me and ease my

tro____no del Si_gnor,
sor____row, gra__cious Lord!

il pian—to mi—o por-ta al
Grant me Thy aid, Ah, ease my

tro—no del Si-gnor, il pian-to mi—o porta al
sor—row, gra-cious Lord! Blind-ed by tears, Rais-ing my

tro—no del Si-gnor, se an cor si pian-ge, si piange in
eyes to the al-might-y God! I implore Thee, Fa-ther, al-might-y

cie—lo, ah il pian-to mi—o reca a'piè del Si-gnor.
Fa—ther, Ah, oh see—me griev—ing! Grant me Thy help, o Lord!

♩ = 100
ALL? MODERATO

ELISABETTA

DON CARLO (*entering*)
È dessa!
Eliz-a-beth!

Un detto, un sol; al
O Car-los, my son, at

UN POCO PIÙ LENTO ♩ = 84

ciel io rac-co-mando il pel-legrin che par-te; e poi sol vi do-
last The hour has come, And you will leave for Flan-ders. And soon your bit-ter

-mando e l'ob-bli-o e la vi-ta.
sor-row Will have fad-ed in o-bliv-ion.

Sì, forte es-ser vo-
Yes, my cour-age will re-

E
D.C
N
No, pensa_te a Ro_
No! Re-mem-ber Rod-
_gl'io; ma quando è infranto a_mo_re, pria del_la morte uc_ci_de.
turn. But once a heart is bro-ken, No cour-age can re-store it.
f
_dri_go. Non è per fol_li i_de_e, ch'ei si sa_cri_fi_cò!
ri-go! 'Tis not for fool-ish dreams That he sac-ri-ficed his life.
Sul_la ter_ra fiam_
On the fields of
pp
(with enthusiasm)
ten.
_min_ga, io vo' che a lui s'innal_zi su_blime, eccelso a_vel, qual mai ne ot_tenne un
Flan-ders I vow to fash-ion him A mon-u-ment so great, so might-y, As has
cres.
ELI.
I. TEMPO ♩ = 100
dolcissimo
I fior del para_di_so a lui sor_ri_de_
Like flow'rs on fra-grant breez_es Our ten-der thoughts will
re tan_to no_bil e bel.
nev-er en-no-bled a king!
I. TEMPO ♩ = 100
p
pp

284

rio, re si i cam - pi un a - vel, un po-po-lo che
blood, Its cur-rent ris-ing high-er,... A peo-ple in de-

muor, e a me la man pro ten-de, sic co-me a Re den-
spair, Their bon-y hands ex-tend-ed, Beg-ging in an-guished

-tor, nei dì del-la sven-tu-ra. A
prayer Their tor-ture may be end-ed. I

lui n'andrò be-a-to, se, spen-to o vin-ci-
lead my peo-ple on-ward, With hon-or to win or

D.C
tor, plauso o pian - to m'a - vrò dal tuo me - mo_re
die, And to find what in hate Here my fate would de-
ff
ELI
MARZIALE 𝅗𝅥=100
(exaltedly)
Sì l'e_ro_i - smo è que - - - sto_e
Bring to your peo - ple_their free - - - dom, Let
D.C
cor!
ny!
Q
MARZIALE 𝅗𝅥=100
ff pp
E
la sua sa_cra fiam - ma! L'amor de - gno di
Free - dom's glo - ry guide you! My love shall ride be -
ff
p
E
noi, l'a - mor che i forti infiam - ma!
side you And brace your daunt - less heart.

287

E
Il po-pol sal - va!
Re deem your peo-ple!
D.C
- la, e, se morrò per lei, la mia morte fia bel - -
ty! Dy - - - ing for you is to drown In an o-cean of beau - -
f
pp
ff
E
Va, va, di più non tar - dar!
Ah! Go, and tar - ry no more!
D.C
- la! Sì mia mor - te fia bel - -
ty! Sing and re - call me to du - -
p
f
E
va, di più non tar dar e salva un po - po - lo che
Go, and tar - ry no more Ride - on to save a land which without you will
D.C
- la! la mia morte fia bel - la!
ty! In an o-cean of beau-ty!
f
pp

Più animato ♩= 126
E
muor!
die!
D.C
Ma pria di que_sto dì al_cun po_ter u_man disgiun_ta non a_
My love, be-fore to-day, No pow'r on earth could part From you, who held in
S
♩= 126
Più animato
p
_vria la mia dal_la tua man!
sway My tor-tured, bro-ken heart:
portando la voce
cres.
ma vin_to in sì gran dì l'onor ha in me l'à_mo_re; im_
Now I have found the key To what my fate in-tend-ed. At
T
ff
p
pp
_pre_sa a questa par rinno_va e men_te e co_re! Non vedi, E_li_sa_
last now my mind is free, And my de-spair is end-ed. E-liz-a-beth, I can be
Più animato

290

E
V
pian - to gli è del - l'alma, e ve-der tu lo
tears of ten - der sor-row, Tears you al - ways will
p
puo-i, qual san pian - to ver - sar - le
find, Where sol - - diers bid fare - well - To
don - ne per gli e - roi!
those who must stay be-hind.
ppp
ASSAI SOSTENUTO ♩ = 60
(solenne) Cantabile
Ma lassù ci vedre - mo in un
But be-yond, up in Heav-en, While its
pp ASSAI SOSTENUTO ♩ = 60
ppp

mon—do mi-glio——re, del—l'av—venir e-
won———ders sur-round us, There, where in love e-

-ter—no suo—nan per noi già l'o——re; e
-ter—nal His might-y will has bound——us, At

là noi tro—ve-rem nel grem—bo del Si-
last He will u-nite And take un-to His

-gnor il sospi-ra-to ben, il so-spi-ra-to ben che fugge in ter-ra o-
heart Those whom the stars had joined, yes whom the stars had joined, But man—has forced a-

293

là noi tro-ve-rem stret-ti in-siem nel Si-
last He will u-nite And en-fold in His

e là noi tro-ve-rem
At last He will u-nite

-gnor e noi là tro-ve-rem stretti insiem nel Si-
heart, He at last will u-nite And en-fold in His

stret-ti insiem nel Signor
And en-fold in His heart

-gnor il so-spi-ra-to ben che fugge in terra o-
heart Those whom the stars had joined, but man has forced a-

il so-spi-ra-to ben, il so-spi-ra-to ben che fug-ge in ter-ra o-
Those whom the stars had joined, yes, whom the stars had joined, But man has forced a-

295

E
D.C
ppp
-fa-ni, tut-ti i no-mi scordiam degli af-fet-ti pro-
sor-row. We re-mem-ber no pain, We re-mem-ber no
-fa-ni, ogni n'ome scordiam degli affet-ti pro-fa-
pain, We re-mem-ber no pain, We re-mem-ber no sor-
CC
-fani. Mio fi-glio, addi-o!
sor-row. I'll think of Car-los,
-ni. Addio, mia ma-dre! E-ter-no ad-
row. Oh, think of Car-los! Leav-ing for-
pp
e-terno addi-o! addi-o! per sempre addi-o! per sem-
Leav-ing for-ev-er! For-ev-er! Leav-ing for-ev-er! For-ev-
-di-o! addi-o! per sempre addi-o! per sempre addi-o! per sem-
ev-er! For-ev-er! Fare-well for-ev-er! Leav-ing for-ev-er! For-ev-
sempre dim.
mf

ALL° AGITATO ♩= 144
E
-pre!
er!
D.C
-pre!
er!
FILIPPO
(taking the Queen by the arm)
Sì, per sempre! Io voglio un doppio sacri-
Yes, for-ev-er! A two-fold sac-ri-fice I
ALL° AGITATO ♩= 144
f
ff
(to the Grand Inquisitor)
F
-fi-zio! Il do-ver mio fa-rò. Ma
of-fer! Now my du-ty is done, And
ELI.
Ciel!
God!
F
voi?
you?
(to the officials of the Inquisition, pointing to Don Carlos)
IL GRANDE INQUISITORE
Il Santo Uf-fi-zio il suo fa-rà. Guardie!
The ho-ly Coun-cil will per-form its task. Guards!
DD
presto

D.CAR. Dio mi vendi- che- rà! il tribunal di
Heav'n will a-venge my death. I shall de-fy your

D.C san- gue sua ma- no spez- ze- rà!
ter- ror Un- til my fi- nal breath.

(Don Carlos, fending off the officials, retreats to the tomb of Charles V.)

(The gate of the tomb opens.)

(The Friar appears recognizable as the former emperor Charles V, wearing his regalia and crown.)

IL FRATE *LARGO COME PRIMA*
Il duo- lo del- la ter- ra nel chio- stro ancor ci
The an- guish of the mor- tal Will e- ven haunt the

LARGO COME PRIMA

se- gue, so- lo del cor la guer- ra in ciel si cal- me-
tem- ple. On- ly the ho- ly por- tal Can grant us fi- nal

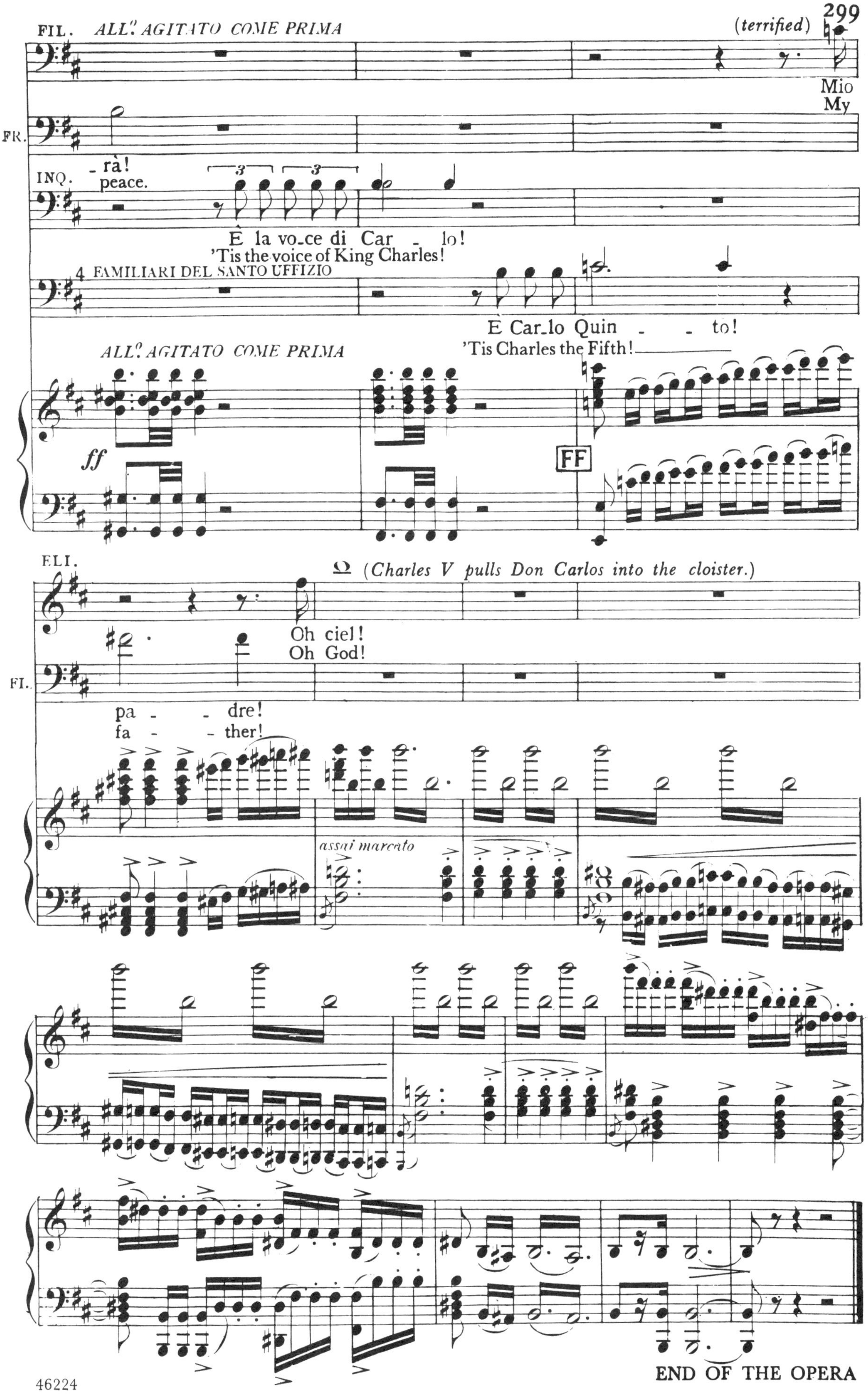

END OF THE OPERA

PA1 contract
Cost of PA
~~Relationship~~ progress with CFBT